Bill and Melinda Gates

FRONT-PAGE LIVES

Bill and Melinda Gates

Sally Isaacs

Heinemann Library
Chicago, IL

J-Biog
G225Ti
Gates

www.heinemannraintree.com
Visit our website to find out more information about Heinemann-Raintree books.

To order:
☎ Phone 888-454-2279
💻 Visit www.heinemannraintree.com to browse our catalog and order online.

Edited by Adam Miller, Andrew Farrow and Adrian Vigliano
Designed by Kimberly Miracle and Betsy Wernert
Picture research by Ruth Blair
Originated by Stephen M. Walker
Printed and Bound in the United States by Corporate Graphics

13 12 11 10
10 9 8 7 6 5 4 3 2

Library of Congress Cataloging-in-Publication Data

Isaacs, Sally Senzell, 1950-
  Bill and Melinda Gates / Sally Isaacs.
    p. cm. -- (Front-page lives)
Includes bibliographical references and index.
  ISBN 978-1-4329-3220-6
1. Gates, Bill, 1955---Juvenile literature. 2. Businesspeople-
-United States--Biography--Juvenile literature. 3. Computer
software industry--United States--History--Juvenile literature.
4. Microsoft Corporation--History--Juvenile literature. 5.
Gates, Melinda, 1964---Juvenile literature. 6. Bill & Melinda
Gates Foundation--History--Juvenile literature. I. Title.
  HD9696.63.U62I83 2010
  338.7'610053092273--dc22
  [B]
                        2009018180

072010
005814RP

Acknowledgments
The author and publishers are grateful to the following for permission to reproduce copyright material:
Alamy/© Chuck Pefley **p.62**; Alamy/© PhotoSpin, Inc **p.56**; Corbis/Bettmann **p.9**; Corbis/Doug Wilson **p.33**; Corbis/Owen Franken **p.45**; Corbis/Reuters **p.71**; Corbis/SIEGEL MIKE/ SEATTLES TIMES **p.64**; Getty Images/Darren McCollester **p.11**; Getty Images/STR/AFP **p.7**; Getty Images/Timothy A Clary/AFP **p.15**; PA Photos **p.19**; PA Photos **p.42**; PA Photos **p.69**; Rex Features/Bolivar Arellano **p.67**; Rex Features/Roger-Viollet; **p.13**; Rex Features/SB/TS/Keystone USA **p.52**; Rex Features/Sipa Press **p.22**; Rex Features/Sipa Press **p.28**; VinMag Archive Ltd **p.35**; Shutterstock background images and design features throughout.

Cover photograph of Melinda and Bill Gates during visit to Manhica Health Research Center in Mozambique reproduced with permission of Corbis/Naashon Zalk

Table of Contents

Some words are shown in bold, **like this**. You can find out what they mean by looking in the glossary.

Great Wealth and Great Responsibility

In some ways Bill and Melinda Gates are just ordinary people. They have three children, whom they drive to school and help with their homework. Yet they are among the most famous, and certainly the richest, people in the world.

Bill's role in starting the Microsoft Corporation, a computer **software** company, made him the world's richest man in 1995, at the very young age of 40. Now he and his wife head the Bill and Melinda Gates **Foundation**. It gives away more money to help others than any other foundation in the world.[1]

THE FOUNDATION

Bill and Melinda Gates travel the world to learn how they can help. In 2006 they visited a poor village in Zambia, in Africa. A deadly disease called **malaria** was killing people in the village. Melinda sat down with some of the mothers. They were especially worried because it had been raining for weeks, and the mosquitoes were swarming terribly. Mosquitoes spread malaria. The mothers explained that they needed nets to cover their children's beds. The nets would keep the mosquitoes from biting their children and spreading the disease. Their families had some nets, but not enough for all the beds.

Melinda was shocked. "How can a mother be forced to make a nightly decision about which child gets to sleep under a bed net, and which child gets bitten?" she recalled in a speech. This was a problem that needed an immediate solution and a long-range plan. She and Bill helped buy bed nets for all the homes. They also gave money to research groups that were trying to find ways to prevent malaria.[2]

The Bill and Melinda Gates Foundation has given more than $17.3 billion to help the least fortunate people in the world.[3] Melinda said, "We go down the chart of the greatest inequities [unfair situations] and give where we can effect the greatest change."[4] The foundation gives money to treat and prevent illness. It also provides **scholarships** to needy students, as well as computers and Internet access to schools and libraries that cannot afford them.

In 2006 Bill Gates said in a speech, "I believe that with great wealth comes great responsibility."[5] This is the story of how Bill and Melinda Gates gained great wealth, and how they are meeting their responsibility by giving back to the world. ❖

December, 2005: Bill and Melinda Gates meet children in the impoverished Meera Bagh slum colony in New Delhi, India. This trip was part of their tour of South Asia, which was focused on improving newborn health, increasing access to immunization, and fighting HIV/AIDS.

Headlines from Bill's Childhood: 1955–1964

Here are some major news stories from the time.

First Humans Launched into Space

Russian astronaut Yuri Gagarin became the first human to be launched into space on April 21, 1961. His spacecraft, *Vostok 1*, lifted off at 9:07 a.m. and spent 108 minutes in flight. The craft made one orbit (circle) of Earth before successfully landing in a field.

On May 5, 1961, 23 days after Gagarin became the first human in space, the United States joined the "space race." Alan B. Shepard, Jr., was the first American to fly in space. Launched by a rocket from Cape Canaveral, Florida, Shepard flew in the *Freedom 7* capsule 187 kilometers (116 miles) above Earth. The capsule did not make a complete orbit. After a flight that lasted 15 minutes and 22 seconds, the capsule splashed down in the Atlantic Ocean.

Crisis Ensues over Soviet Missiles

On October 14, 1962, U.S. spy planes discovered that the **Soviet Union** was setting up bases for nuclear weapons in Cuba, just 90 miles (145 kilometers) from the coast of Florida. The reports estimated that the missiles were capable of reaching several major U.S. cities.

The world seemed on the brink of a nuclear war. It was the height of the **Cold War**. The United States and Soviet Union were locked in an economic and political struggle between **communism** and **capitalism**. On October 22, President John F. Kennedy warned the Soviet leader, Nikita Khrushchev, to remove the missiles. He warned that any missiles fired from Cuba would be met with an attack on the Soviet Union.

On October 28, after a 13-day standoff, Khrushchev announced that the weapons would be removed in return for a U.S. agreement not to invade communist Cuba. Secretly, Kennedy also promised to remove U.S. missiles located in Turkey.

Civil Rights Protesters March on Washington, D.C.

On August 28, 1963, an estimated 200,000 people gathered in front of the Lincoln Memorial in Washington, D.C., to demand an end to racial segregation in the United States. Protestors demanded that all Americans have equal rights, no matter their skin color. The last of the speakers, Martin Luther King, Jr., electrified the crowd with a nationally televised speech that became known as "I Have a Dream."

President Kennedy Assassinated

On November 22, 1963, at the age of 43, U.S. President John F. Kennedy was assassinated. Three years earlier, he had become the youngest person ever elected president of the United States. On the day of the shooting, Kennedy and his wife, Jacqueline, were riding in the backseat of a convertible through Dallas, Texas, on the way to a political luncheon. Crowds of people lined the streets to greet them. Suddenly, shots rang out from a seven-story building. Two bullets struck Kennedy in the head and neck, and his car sped off to a hospital. Within an hour, the president was pronounced dead. That same afternoon, police found and arrested the man believed to be the shooter, Lee Harvey Oswald. Meanwhile, aboard the presidential plane heading back to Washington, D.C., Vice President Lyndon B. Johnson was sworn in as the next president of the United States.

President Kennedy with his wife Jacqueline, shortly before he was shot.

Getting Started

Bill Gates was born on October 28, 1955, in Seattle, Washington. His real name is William Henry Gates, III. Bill was the third William H. Gates in his family, so his grandmother nicknamed him Trey. Trey is a card-playing term for "three."[1]

Bill was not the first person in his family with a keen business sense. In 1898 his great-grandfather moved his family from Seattle to Nome, Alaska, to sell furniture to miners during the gold rush. Bill's grandfather started his own community newspaper there when he was just eight years old. The family later moved back to Seattle, where Bill's dad was born. Bill's dad started his own local newspaper when he was 13. His name is William H. Gates II, or Bill Senior. He later became a lawyer.[2]

Bill's mother was named Mary Maxwell Gates. She was a schoolteacher. She gave up teaching to raise her family and volunteer for **charitable** organizations. She became chairwoman of United Way International, an organization that helps local groups that work with people in need.[3]

CHILDHOOD

Bill was the middle child in the family, between his older sister, Kristianne, and his younger sister, Libby. Ever since he was a young boy, Bill loved to compete in games and contests. Even more, he loved to win. After dinner, the family dove into trivia contests, jigsaw puzzles, and card games. Losers had to do the dishes. Young Bill also loved to read and figure things out. Sometimes he lost track of time. He often kept his family waiting when they were ready to go someplace. They would call out, "What are you doing?" Bill would reply, "I'm thinking. I'm thinking."

By the age of nine, Bill had read an entire set of encyclopedias. He was a smart boy, but he did not have an easy time at View Ridge Elementary School. His October birthday made him the youngest person in his class. He was also the smallest. He was full of energy and could not keep himself busy enough. Though he was left-handed, sometimes he took notes with his right hand, just to give himself a challenge. He earned As in math and reading, but Cs and Ds in handwriting, citizenship, and other subjects that he did not think were important.[4]

Bill and Melinda Gates (left) pose with Bill's father, Bill Sr., and stepmother, Mimi, at Harvard University in 2007. Bill Sr. married Mimi in 1996, two years after the death of Mary Maxwell Gates, the mother of Bill, Kristianne, and Libby.

A GLIMPSE OF THE FUTURE

In the 1950s and 1960s, when Bill Gates was a young boy, people did not have computers in their homes. Computers were used in banks and in universities for scientific research. These computers were so large that one of them could fill an entire room.

In 1962, when Bill was six years old, his parents took him to the Seattle World's Fair. These fairs are held every few years in different cities worldwide. Like all fairs, they have food and rides. They also have large exhibits from various countries as well as displays of the latest technology.

Bill loved the mile-long monorail train and the exciting Wild Mouse roller coaster. When he entered the technology exhibits, he took his first step into the world of computers. The American Library Association displayed its giant UNIVAC computer (see panel below). It was the size of a one-car garage. This enormous computer was slower and held much less information than today's computers. However, it calculated numbers and sorted information much faster than people could without a computer. This UNIVAC held information from about 8,400 books, quotes from 74 authors, and statistics on 92 nations. At the exhibit,

UNIVAC

UNIVAC stands for "Universal Automatic Computer." The first one was invented in 1951. It was used by the U.S. Bureau of Census to keep track of the number of people living in the country. In 1952 it was used to keep track of the results of the U.S. presidential election. Just 45 minutes after the polls closed, UNIVAC predicted that Dwight D. Eisenhower had won the election. It was correct![5]

The ENIAC computer, 1946. The ENIAC computer was an earlier invention by the same people who later created UNIVAC. ENIAC stands for "Electronic Numerical Integrator and Computer" and was the first large, general-purpose, electronic computer. ENIAC was invented during World War II in a secret military project known as Project PX.

visitors presented questions to a librarian. The computer searched its store of information and spewed out the answers. Everyone, including Bill, was amazed.[6]

IMAGINING THE FUTURE

The 1962 World's Fair was known as "Century 21." Many exhibits showed what experts predicted for the future—in the year 2001. Some of the predictions did not come true. We still do not travel on supersonic airplanes that zip around the globe in minutes, and we do not wear rocket belts that "enable a man to stride 30 feet" (9 meters).

Other predictions are here today. These include cordless telephones and movies that can be watched as soon as they are filmed. The "office of the future" had machines that sent and received messages, as ours do today. The "home of the future" had computers to help with shopping, writing checks, and keeping records.[7]

No one at the World's Fair could have predicted that Bill Gates would play a big part in the future of computers. Just six years later, when he was 12 years old, he sat in front of a computer **terminal** for the first time. That is when he would begin to meet his future.

MELINDA FRENCH

When Bill was eight years old, Melinda French was born in Dallas, Texas. She had a very typical childhood with her older sister and two younger brothers. Her father, Raymond French, Jr., was an **engineer** who worked on the U.S. space program. Melinda's mother, Elaine Amerland French, stayed at home and took care of the children. Melinda's father earned extra income by renting out small homes he owned to other people. On the weekends, Melinda's whole family pitched in to get these homes ready to rent. They scrubbed floors, mowed lawns, and cleaned ovens.[8]

Melinda and Bill grew up more than 2,000 miles (3,220 kilometers) apart. They were eight years apart in age. Years later, in 1986, they would meet and find that they had many things in common.

A NEW HOME FOR BILL

In the middle of fourth grade, Bill's family moved a few miles away from Seattle, to Laurelhurst, Washington. They had a bigger home in a nicer neighborhood. Bill finished his elementary school years at Laurelhurst Elementary School. He joined the Contemporary Club, which was a

Melinda French grew up many miles from Bill Gates, and was eight years younger than him. However, when they finally met in 1986, they found that they had much in common.

group of smart students who met to talk about books and current events and to take field trips to museums. Some of Bill's teachers thought he was **obsessive**. When he worked on something, he did not want to stop. His fourth-grade teacher assigned a four-page report on the human body. Bill wrote more than thirty pages.[9]

During the summer, Bill enjoyed swimming, diving, roller-skating, and tennis. He was competitive and liked to keep moving. Baseball was too slow for him. His mind wandered in between the pitches.[10]

OUTDOOR FUN

Bill loved being a Boy Scout, especially activities such as hiking and camping. On one camping trip, the troop's tents were flooded by a downpour. While most of the boys huddled together under a plastic tarp, Bill and a friend stayed in their collapsed tent and laughed through the storm. Bill took pride in winning awards for the dirtiest clothes at the end of the hikes. More seriously, he earned many merit badges. Scouts earn merit badges by doing a list of required tasks for various subjects, such as nature, art, and business.

Every year, Bill's family spent two weeks at a waterfront camp in Washington called Cheerio. Many families vacationed there. Bill and his friends organized games they called the Cheerio Olympics. These included egg tosses and three-legged races. They carried out elaborate Olympic-like rituals, including opening ceremonies, a torch lighting, and medal presentations.[11]

Bill's parents could afford to give their children many things, but they also encouraged them to earn money. Bill earned a few dollars a week delivering newspapers. His parents also taught the children to share what they had with others. At the dinner table, Bill Sr. and Mary talked about their work with charitable organizations and people who were less fortunate than the Gates family. Bill and his sisters gave a portion of the allowances they received to help others.[12] ❖

Melinda's life

Many books and articles tell about Bill Gates's childhood. But there is not much information about Melinda's childhood. She is a private person. When she started dating Bill, reporters tried to interview her schoolteachers and friends. She asked them not to share information about her life. In recent years, though, she has agreed to be interviewed by the media.[13]

HEADLINES FROM BILL'S SCHOOL YEARS: 1965–1972

Here are some major news stories from the time.

The Six-Day War Begins

In 1967 tensions were high in Israel and its surrounding countries. Ever since Israel was founded in 1948, Arab states, including Egypt, Jordan, and Syria, had refused to accept Israel as an independent state. Israel and many people from these Arab states claimed the land as their homeland. Beginning on June 5, air attacks between Israel and the Arab states turned into all-out war. In six days, Israel drove the Arab army out of the disputed land. It also reunited Jerusalem by taking control of the eastern half, which had been under Jordanian control.

First Human Heart Transplant Performed

Medical history was made on December 3, 1967, when South African surgeon Christiaan Barnard performed the first human-to-human heart transplant surgery. The heart of a 25-year-old woman who died in a car accident was transplanted into the body of a 53-year-old man dying from heart disease. While the surgery was successful, the man died 18 days later from pneumonia.

Men Land on the Moon!

On July 20, 1969, U.S. astronauts Neil Armstrong and Buzz Aldrin became the first two humans to set foot on the Moon. The world watched on television as Armstrong took the first step and announced: "That's one small step for [a] man, one giant leap for mankind."

Sesame Street Debuts

On November 10, 1969, children everywhere were introduced to large, lovable Muppets (puppets) named Big Bird, Bert, Ernie, Grover, and Cookie Monster. These were the stars of a new television hit called Sesame Street. The show appealed to adults and kids. It has remained on the air for more than 40 years.

Tallest Buildings in World Constructed in Manhattan

Architect Minoru Yamasaki began construction on the ambitious World Trade Center project in 1966. When they were complete, the "Twin Towers" were 110 floors and reached heights of over 1,360 feet (415 meters). The buildings stayed the tallest in the world until the Sears Tower opened in Chicago in 1973. The "Twin Towers" remained a prominent fixture of the New York City skyline unitl the morning of September 11, 2001.

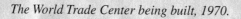

The World Trade Center being built, 1970.

The Beatles Break Up

On April 10, 1970, Paul McCartney publicly announced that the enormously popular band, the Beatles, was splitting up. The British foursome, also including John Lennon, George Harrison, and Ringo Starr, began performing in 1961. They became one of the most successful, internationally famous bands ever. Their music and mop-head hairstyles took the young music scene by storm. People called it "Beatlemania." After eighteen very popular albums, four movies, and countless hysterical concerts, the group decided to split. The members continued to perform and record individually.

School Days

When Bill Gates was 11 years old, his parents worried about his attitude toward school. He did not pay attention to his teachers. His desk was always messy. He studied for tests at the last minute, if at all. Gates's parents desperately wanted him to build some good study habits.

They decided to send him to a private school called Lakeside School. It was a serious school for grades seven through twelve. When Gates started at Lakeside, it was an all-boys school. Students had to wear jackets and ties and carry their books and papers in briefcases. They sat in assigned seats for lunch.

In seventh grade, Gates's report card had mostly Bs, with an A-minus in an algebra honors class. Clearly Gates was very smart, but some kids thought he was a show-off. For example, when he volunteered to explain a math problem, he filled every inch of the board with numbers. But there were other math whiz kids in the school, and they became his friends.[1]

GATES MEETS THE COMPUTER

The Lakeside Mothers' Club donated money to buy a computer terminal for the school. The terminal was connected by telephone lines to a refrigerator-sized **mainframe** computer owned by General Electric in downtown Seattle. A mainframe is a very large, powerful computer. This one was a **PDP-10** made by the DEC company. Several businesses and universities shared this computer. People paid each time they sat at their terminals and connected to the PDP-10. This was called **time sharing**. At first, the Mothers' Club paid for the students' time on the computer. Later, the boys would have to pay for the time themselves.[2]

Lakeside was one of the first schools in the country to have computer power. One of Lakeside's math teachers taught the boys what he knew about a computer language called **BASIC**. It stands for "Beginner's All-Purpose Symbolic Instruction Code." The boys used the language to write software. Software is a program that tells a computer what to do. The physical parts of the computer are called the **hardware**.[3]

"We were too young to drive or to do any of the other fun-seeming adult activities, but we could give this machine orders and it would always obey."
—Bill Gates

AN OBSESSION

A group of boys flocked to the computer immediately, including the youngest and smallest, 12-year-old Bill Gates. They poured over the computer manual and figured out new ways to make the computer work. At this time, Gates became good friends with three boys who would play special roles in his life. Kent Evans and Richard Weiland were in seventh grade with Gates. Paul Allen was in tenth grade. To all these boys, the computer was more than a hobby. It was an obsession. With any spare minutes, they ran to the computer room and wrote programs. One of their first programs was for a tic-tac-toe game.

In 1995 Gates wrote a book called *The Road Ahead*. In it, he described why he loved the computer:

> We were too young to drive or to do any of the other fun-seeming adult activities, but we could give this machine orders and it would always obey. . . That was the beginning of my fascination with software. . . And to this day it still thrills me to know that if I can get the program right it will always work perfectly, every time, just the way I told it to.[4]

Paul Allen (left) and Bill Gates (right), 1981. Gates and Allen bonded in high school over their love of computers. A few years later, they would turn their hobby into what would become a multi-billion dollar company.

C-CUBED

General Electric charged $40 an hour for computer time. The Mothers' Club had donated $3,000 to pay for the computer time, but the boys used that time within a few weeks. After that, each boy had to pay his own way. Gates's parents insisted that he use his own money for this. Luckily a computer company came along and offered to help him.[5]

Computer Center Corporation, also known as C-Cubed, was a new company that sold time shares on a new DEC PDP-10 computer. In those early days, computers usually crashed, or stopped working, after a half hour. The company needed people with computer skills to test their computers, check for bugs, and see what made them crash. A C-Cubed employee named Monique Rona, who was the mother of a Lakeside student, came up with an idea. The company could put the Lakeside boys to work. The boys could have all the computer time they wanted by coming to C-Cubed and testing the computer. It was a dream come true for Bill Gates and his friends.[6]

FIRST JOBS

Every Saturday morning, Gates and his friends happily arrived at the C-Cubed office to work on the PDP-10. The boys' main job was to make the computer crash and then find out why. What a great assignment!

Before long, the boys started going to C-Cubed after school in addition to Saturdays. Gates often brought C-Cubed work home, filling his room with stacks of papers. Sometimes, after bedtime, he sneaked out of the house and rode a bus back to C-Cubed to program some more.[7]

By ninth grade, Gates's parents felt he was addicted to the computer. They ordered him to stay away from computers for a while. He did that for almost a year during 9th and 10th grades.[8]

Without the computer, Gates spent more time reading books. He enjoyed reading biographies and science fiction, as well as business and science books. His favorite books were *The Catcher in the Rye* and *A Separate Peace*.[9]

LEARNING LANGUAGES

In October 1970, Gates turned 15 and was in 10th grade. He returned from his "computer break" and desperately wanted free computer time. He was also sharpening his business skills. He knew that he and his friends had experience with computers that most people did not have. Why not earn money with these valuable skills?

Gates, Allen, Weiland, and Evans formed a business called the Lakeside Programmers Group. They lined up some work through Allen's dad at the University of Washington. Then a company called Information Systems Incorporated (ISI) hired them to write a program that kept track of employee paychecks. ISI did not want the program written in BASIC language. They wanted it written in a language that most businesses used called COBOL, which stands for "Common Business-Oriented Language" (see box). The boys taught themselves COBOL, adding another valuable skill to their list.[10]

TRAF-O-DATA

While Gates was still at Lakeside, Paul Allen went to college in Pullman, Washington. The two boys remained good friends. Allen was fascinated by computer hardware. Gates just wanted to write software. They made a great team.

In 1972, when Gates was 16 and Allen was 19, Allen noticed a small article in *Popular Electronics* magazine. It talked about a new company called Intel and its new **microprocessor** called the 8008. A microprocessor is small chip that holds the "brains" of the computer. Gates and Allen were thrilled. They pooled money that each of them had saved and went to an electronics store, where they bought the 8008 chip for $360. It came in a little paper box, wrapped in aluminum foil and a

Computer languages

People use computer languages to write software, the programs that tell a computer what to do. BASIC was one of the first and most common computer languages. It may be the easiest language to learn. COBOL is better for processing business information. FORTRAN is good for scientific and complicated mathematic problems.

Below is the beginning part of a BASIC program which gives a computer instructions for finding the average of a list of numbers:

```
10 SUM = 0
20 READ LENGTH
30 COUNTER = LENGTH.

40  READ NEXT

50 SUM = SUM + NEXT

60 IF COUNTER = 1 GOTO 90

70 COUNTER = COUNTER - 1

80 GOTO 40

90 AVG ==2 0SUM/LENGTH

100 PRINT AVG

110 DATA 7, 35, 9000, 876, 29, 87, 90, 153

120 END [11]
```

piece of foam plastic. Compared to today's standards, the chip was not very advanced. But they were eager to write software for it.[12]

Allen and Gates designed a program to help cities understand the traffic flow in different locations. Many cities lay rubber hoses across selected streets. As a car crosses over the hose, the force punches a paper tape, which is in a box at the end of the hose. Gates and Allen created a computer program to analyze the data on the tape. The program would print out graphs and other statistics. Gates and Allen created their own company and called it Traf-O-Data. They made a few sales of the Traf-O-Data machines, but not nearly as many as they wanted.[13]

A TRAGIC ACCIDENT

In the middle of Gates's junior year, the Lakeside teachers offered him a job using the computer to organize class schedules. Lakeside had merged with the all-girls St. Nicholas School, and it was a challenge to arrange all the class schedules. The old system of pinning index cards onto a wall was not working. Gates and his friend Kent Evans agreed to do the job. They spent hours in the computer room. Sometimes they slept there overnight.[14]

The project came to a tragic halt on May 28, 1972. Seventeen-year-old Evans was hiking with a mountaineering class. He tripped and fell 800 feet (250 meters) and later died on board a rescue helicopter. Gates and his friends were heartbroken about losing Evans. But when Paul Allen returned from college, he helped Gates finish the scheduling program.[15] ❖

The First E-mail Is Sent

In the 1960s a bright computer engineer named Ray Tomlinson was hired to work on a new communications network called ARPANET. Through ARPANET, scientists and other researchers could share one another's computer facilities. In his work, Tomlinson discovered that computer users in different locations could send their files to one another. In designing electronic "names" for the users, Tomlinson chose the @ sign to connect the name and address. In October 1971 Tomlinson sent the first e-mail message to himself at a separate location. He did not recall the message, but thought it might have been something like "testing 1-2-3."

HEADLINES FROM THE COLLEGE YEARS: 1973–1978

Here are some major news stories from the time.

The evacuation of Saigon, April 20, 1975. A U.S. Marine helicopter rescues people from the roof of the embassy.

The Vietnam War Ends

On January 15, 1973, U.S. President Richard Nixon ordered a stop to U.S. military operations in Vietnam, a country in Southeast Asia. Since the 1950s, there had been fighting between communist-run North Vietnam and the government of South Vietnam. The United States sent military and civilian personnel to help South Vietnam and stop the spread of communism. Australia, New Zealand, the Philippines, South Korea, and Thailand also helped this cause. By 1969 there were about 540,000 U.S. troops in Vietnam. They were fighting North Vietnamese soldiers, as well as guerilla fighters called the Viet Cong, who were backed by the North. U.S. citizens protested the war in massive demonstrations throughout the country. President Nixon ordered a stop to military operations. The last U.S. troops left Vietnam on March 29, 1973. The war resumed, but U.S. troops did not return. The war ended on April 30, 1975, when South Vietnam surrendered to North Vietnam.

Arab–Israeli Conflict Leads to Oil Crisis

As part of a continuing battle over land (see page 18), Egypt and Syria attacked Israel during Israel's holiest day, Yom Kippur. This triggered yet another Arab–Israeli War, which lasted from October 6 to October 25, 1973. In the end, no land actually changed hands.

The United States sent weapons and money for Israel's defense. As punishment, oil-producing Arab nations called for an oil embargo. This official order stopped the shipment of oil to the United States. It also raised the price of oil worldwide. Americans found themselves in long lines for gasoline. They paid almost double the former price for gasoline and heating oil. The U.S. secretary of state, Henry Kissinger, traveled between Israel and Syria to try to negotiate a settlement of their conflict. By March 1974 Israel agreed to withdraw from parts of the disputed Sinai peninsula. With that, the Arab oil producers lifted the embargo.

VCRs Are Introduced

In 1975 the Sony Corporation introduced a home videotape system from its headquarters in Japan. Its format was called Betamax. In 1976 a company called JVC introduced its recording system in a VHS format. Though Betamax and VHS had similar technology, they were different sizes. Consumers were slow to buy either machine at first. Gradually VHS won out, and videocassette recorders became as popular as television sets.

A Science Fiction Hit Debuts

On May 25, 1977, movie fans lined up for an action-packed science fiction movie, *Star Wars*, written and directed by George Lucas. It is about a character named Luke Skywalker (Mark Hamill) who meets a warrior (Alec Guinness), a pilot (Harrison Ford), and two scene-stealing robots named R2-D2 and C3-PO. Together they fight galactic enemies and free the rebel leader, Princess Leia (Carrie Fisher). The movie later won Academy Awards for its music, costumes, art direction, film editing, and—its most memorable feature—special effects.

Heading to Harvard

In 1972, the summer before his senior year at Lakeside, Gates was 16 years old and working as a congressional page in Washington, D.C. Congressional pages run errands for members of the Senate and House of Representatives. They deliver documents and do office work. Gates was glad that Congressman Brock Adams, a friend of his parents, recommended him to be a page.

By his senior year, everyone at Lakeside knew Bill Gates. He was the smartest kid in school, and the one who could answer the hardest trick questions in class. He could make people laugh with his sarcastic humor. He could make them angry by teasing them when they answered questions too slowly. He was the kid who started arguments with the teachers. Though he wasn't paid much as a congressional page, he was beginning to make some money through his other work. He was the kid who drove the shiny red Mustang and—just for fun—pulled out a thousand-dollar bill to pay for a cheeseburger at a teen hangout.[1]

A NEW OPPORTUNITY

In the middle of Gates's senior year, he received a surprising phone call. A business called TRW in Vancouver, Washington, had a power-company project that was way behind schedule and full of computer bugs. They needed programmers who were familiar with DEC computers. These were the kind of computers Gates knew from his work at Information

Systems Incorporated (ISI). One of TRW's managers had worked with Gates and Paul Allen at ISI when Gates was in 10th grade. The manager wanted them to move to Vancouver and work on this TRW project.[2]

Allen wanted the job so much that he dropped out of college. Gates wanted to grab the opportunity, too. This was a chance to work with more computers than ever and to learn from experienced programmers. Gates asked Lakeside for permission to skip the rest of his senior year. He asked the school to give him credit for the TRW work as a "senior project." He promised to return for graduation. The school agreed.[3]

Gates loved the TRW job. He got to work in a huge control room filled with computers, maps, grids, and flashing lights. His assignments were not exciting. He sat at a computer all day and wrote down every error message. Still, he was thrilled to be there.[4]

As promised, Gates went home for graduation and the senior prom. He asked a Lakeside junior—Melissa Kristoferson—to be his prom date. In 1973 teenagers enjoyed the idea of a senior prom, but they experimented with ways to be different. At the prom, Gates dressed up in a white frock coat, pink ruffled shirt, top hat, and cane.[5]

COLLEGE LIFE

Gates applied to several top colleges in the United States: Harvard, Princeton, and Yale. He was accepted by all three. The admissions officers probably were impressed with his work experience at computer companies, his good grades in advanced classes, and his perfect score on the math SAT.[6] The SAT is a test that is supposed to predict how well a student will perform in college classes. Gates chose to attend Harvard, near Boston, Massachusetts. In the fall of 1973, he started his freshman year. Before Gates started, Allen warned him, "There are going to be some guys at Harvard who are smarter than you." Gates replied, "No way!"[7]

> ## *"There are going to be some guys at Harvard who are smarter than you."*
> —Paul Allen
>
> ## *"No way!"*
> —Bill Gates

Harvard was not easy. Gates stayed up all night working on math problems. He got Ds on his first chemistry exams. As he did in high school, Gates eventually raised his grades to As.[8] However, he was a serious **procrastinator**. He put off doing things that he had to do. He skipped classes and never studied. Then before a test, he stayed up all night to get the work done. Gates regretted this habit later when he was in charge of his own company. Some of his first software customers were Japanese businessmen. They were so concerned about Gates completing their project that they flew over from Japan to watch him work![9]

Gates took classes in math, literature, psychology, economics, and history. But he was happiest in Harvard's Aiken Computer Center, working at its PDP computers. The center was reserved for upperclassmen, but Gates begged a professor to let him in. For an end-of-year project, he worked through the nights on a computer baseball game. In true Gates style, it became very complicated. He wanted the pitcher to throw a ball and the field figure to bend down to pick up a ball. In those days, such graphics were unheard of. By the end of the year, he was disappointed in the game.[10]

Gates did not date much during college. When he went back to Seattle on school vacations, he sometimes went out with a family friend named Karen Gloyd. He never was very smooth at starting conversations with

Though Bill Gates took classes in math, literature, psychology, economics, and history, he felt most comfortable behind a computer. He often put off work on other subjects, but was happy to spend long nights creating complicated computer programs.

girls. When he met Gloyd, he immediately asked her about her SAT scores. Then he went on to talk for a long time about his own scores. Gloyd thought he was smart and nice, but shy and inexperienced with girls.[11]

MELINDA FRENCH IN ELEMENTARY SCHOOL

As Gates was starting Harvard, his future wife, Melinda French, attended St. Monica Elementary School in Dallas, Texas. Her favorite subject was math. In those days, many parents did not encourage their daughters to have careers, especially in math and science. Melinda's parents, however, celebrated her good math grades. Melinda once explained, "I had parents who told me every step of the way, 'You can get what you want.'"[12]

ANOTHER SUPER CHIP

During Gates's freshman year, Paul Allen started a new programming job in Boston. The two friends now lived close to each other again. They spent many weekends and evenings together working at a computer or reading electronics magazines. They wanted to learn everything about new computer technology. Gates and Allen predicted, or at least hoped, that people would eventually own **personal computers (PCs)**. These would be small, less expensive desktop computers used by one person at a time. Gates later wrote, "I'm sure that one of the reasons I was so determined to help develop the personal computer is that I wanted one for myself."[13]

In the spring of 1974, they saw an article in *Popular Electronics* magazine that seemed to prove they could be right. Intel announced a new 8080 microprocessor chip. It was 10 times more powerful than the 8008 chip that Gates and Allen put in their Traf-O-Data machines. The price of the chip was under $200.[14]

This was big news! Computer companies could start building smaller computers that used this microprocessor chip. There was no more need for **time sharing** on big, refrigerator-sized machines. More people could

Popular Electronics

WORLD'S LARGEST-SELLING ELECTRONICS MAGAZINE   JANUARY 1975/75¢

PROJECT BREAKTHROUGH!

World's First Minicomputer Kit to Rival Commercial Models...

"ALTAIR 8800"   SAVE OVER $1000

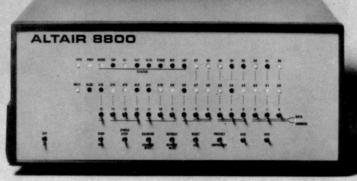

ALTAIR 8800

ALSO IN THIS ISSUE:

- An Under-$90 Scientific Calculator Project
- CCD's—TV Camera Tube Successor?
- Thyristor-Controlled Photoflashers

TEST REPORTS:

Technics 200 Speaker System
Pioneer RT-1011 Open-Reel Recorder
Tram Diamond-
Edmund Scienti
Hewlett-Packa

18101

The January 1975 issue of Popular Electronics *magazine was very exciting for people like Gates and Allen. The magazine introduced the world to the first "minicomputer kit." (See pages 37–38.)*

> *"I'm sure that one of the
> reasons I was so determined to
> help develop the personal computer
> is that I wanted one for myself."*
> —Bill Gates, talking about his interest
> in computers during college

afford computers, and there were endless possibilities for using them. Gates and Allen saw this as a business opportunity. As Gates started his sophomore year at Harvard in the fall of 1974, he and Allen sent letters from Gates's dorm room to all the big computer companies. They offered to write programs for the 8080 chip. No one replied. Apparently the computer companies were not as excited about the chip as Gates and Allen were.[15]

Gates continued to take a variety of classes. He was never sure what he wanted to major in. When he started at Harvard, he thought he might become a lawyer like his father. Then he thought he might be a math teacher. In his heart, he knew his career had to be connected to the world of computers.

AN UNLIKELY FRIEND

Gates made a lifelong friend during his sophomore year at Harvard. Steve Ballmer lived down the hall from Gates in a dorm called Currier House. Ballmer was a friendly guy who loved to be with lots of people. He joined all kinds of groups, from the football team to the school newspaper. Gates was the opposite. He was more of a loner, preferring small groups of friends. Even though they had opposite personalities, the two friends shared a high energy level. They stayed up all night talking, arguing, and laughing. Much later, in 2000, Gates would choose Ballmer to be the **chief executive officer (CEO)** of his company, Microsoft.[16]

THE ALTAIR ARRIVES

One freezing January morning in 1975, Gates and Allen passed a newsstand and saw an amazing magazine cover. The January issue of *Popular Electronics* showed a photograph of a computer the size of a toaster oven. It was the "world's first minicomputer kit," called the Altair 8800 (see box). It used the Intel 8080 microprocessor chip. Though the computer arrived in pieces and could not do much, this was the forerunner of the personal computer that Gates and Allen dreamed about.[17]

Altair 8800

The Altair 8800 appealed to people who build and use computers for a hobby. The Altair 8800 had no keyboard or display screen. There were 16 lights and 16 switches that directed the commands. A user could enter a program by flipping switches. Some of the first applications were simple games such as Hangman and Hammurabi and games inspired by *Star Trek*. The kit cost $397, but that was without any memory or software. All that cost extra.[19]

A company called Micro Instrumentation and Telemetry Systems (MITS), in Albuquerque, New Mexico, developed the Altair 8800. In 1971 MITS had become successful by introducing an electronic calculator kit. Now it hoped for another winner with the Altair computer kit. Soon after the Altair appeared on the magazine cover, thousands of orders flooded into MITS. Before then, people who wanted to build computers had to shop around for every bulb, chip, and switch. Now all the parts came in one box. And once they put all the pieces together, people had a computer for a pretty low price. But it did not come with any software. After turning it on, the user had to "boot" it by flipping switches hundreds of different ways. The computer was not able to do computer work as we know it today, but it was an exciting breakthrough for die-hard computers buffs. Gates and Allen were two of those people.[18]

"Writing good software requires a lot of concentration, and writing BASIC for the Altair was exhausting. Sometimes I rock back and forth or pace when I'm thinking because it helps me focus on a single idea and exclude distractions. I did a lot of rocking and pacing in my dorm room the winter of 1975."
—Bill Gates

WRITING SOFTWARE

The new personal computers became known as **microcomputers**. A microcomputer is a small computer that uses a single microprocessor chip. When the Altair 8800 came along, no one had developed a simple language, like BASIC, for microcomputers. The machines used high-level languages that most people would find too complicated. Gates and Allen wanted to create simpler BASIC software for microcomputers. Now they could start with this Altair. They decided not to buy the Altair kit. Instead, Allen studied a manual for the 8080 chip. Then they wrote a program for one of the big Harvard computers to make it act like the tiny Altair. This let them use their familiar computer to test their new software.[20]

Gates and Allen worked around the clock on the software. Sometimes they forgot to eat and sleep. Gates described this experience in his book

The Road Ahead: "Writing good software requires a lot of concentration, and writing BASIC for the Altair was exhausting. Sometimes I rock back and forth or pace when I'm thinking because it helps me focus on a single idea and exclude distractions. I did a lot of rocking and pacing in my dorm room the winter of 1975." Finally, after five weeks, they finished their program. It could perform simple math calculations.[21]

MICRO-SOFT

Gates and Allen wrote a letter to Ed Roberts, the president of MITS, the company that developed the Altair 8800. They wanted to sell him BASIC software for the Altair. Roberts could buy it from them and sell it to MITS customers. Roberts agreed to look at the program. Soon Allen flew to Albuquerque, New Mexico. He was more than a little nervous. He had never run his program on a real Altair, and he did not know if it would work. Roberts gave Allen a quick tour of MITS and showed him the Altair. Allen took a deep breath and typed the instructions: "PRINT 2+2." The Altair printed out the answer: 4. Roberts was amazed—and, frankly, Allen was, too. Roberts offered jobs to both Allen and Gates.[22]

With this news, Gates and Allen decided to form the world's first microcomputer software company. In 1976 they officially named it Micro-Soft, a combination of *microcomputer* and *software*. In 1979 they dropped the hyphen in the name to become Microsoft.[23]

LEAVING HARVARD

Allen moved to Albuquerque to be the director of software development at MITS. Gates worked on the MITS software from Harvard. He spent his summers in Albuquerque.

In 1975, at just 19 years old, Gates decided to leave Harvard. He was only a junior, with another year before graduation. However, he believed he needed to work full time for Microsoft before competitors jumped ahead of him. Gates talked about his decision to leave college with his parents. They were concerned, but they finally supported his decision. He planned to return to his studies later, but he never did (see box).

In 1976 Microsoft set up its first official office. It was on the eighth floor of a bank building near the Albuquerque airport.[24]

Reflections on dropping out

Many years later, after Gates became a billionaire, he wrote about leaving college:

> It concerns me to hear young people say they don't want to go to college because I didn't graduate. For one thing, I got a pretty good education even though I didn't stay long enough to get my degree. . . . I loved my years at college and, in many respects, I regretted leaving. I did it only because I had an idea—founding the first microcomputer software company— that couldn't wait.[25]

LIVING IN ALBUQUERQUE

Gates moved to Albuquerque and shared an apartment with Allen. Soon they both decided they wanted to branch out from MITS. New computer companies were opening every day, including Apple, Tandy, and Radio Shack. Gates and Allen wanted them all to use Microsoft software.

Gates and Allen shifted into new roles as business managers. They hired some high school friends to work on programming. They met with lawyers to write contracts with the computer companies. The companies created licensing agreements with Microsoft. These agreements would allow them to load software onto their computers after paying Microsoft a fee to do this.[26]

THE KEYS TO SUCCESS

Though Gates was just 20 and looked like a scruffy kid, he already had three traits of a successful businessperson. First, he had vision. He looked at what was happening with computers and predicted that more and more people would be buying them. He also predicted that software would be as important to computers as gasoline is to cars. That is why he decided to build a software business. Second, Gates had confidence. He was sure that with hard work and skilled employees, anything was possible. Third, he set high standards. He demanded the best work from himself and his staff. ❖

HEADLINES FROM MICROSOFT'S EARLY YEARS: 1979–1984

Here are some major news stories from the time.

Nuclear Leak Occurs in Pennsylvania

On March 28, 1979, thousands of people fled their homes after learning about an accident at the nuclear power plant at Three Mile Island, near Middletown, Pennsylvania. They feared a nuclear explosion. Nuclear explosions send dangerous radioactive particles into the air and water. This can make people sick or die. The explosion did not happen. However, some radioactive water and gases were released. Several agencies concluded that there were no negative health effects in the people or animals in the area. Still, the incident led to stricter rules for nuclear reactor sites, better training of the personnel, and increased public criticism of nuclear power.

The Three Mile Island nuclear leak occured after a water pump broke down at the plant. Though this caused the plant's reactor to automatically shut down, it did not prevent radioactive steam from leaking into the air. Luckily, nobody died in the accident, which was eventually blamed on a combination of human error and equipment failure.

The Olympic Games Are Boycotted

Cold War tension between the United States and the Soviet Union drifted into the sports world. To protest the Soviet Union's recent invasion of Afghanistan, the United States refused to send athletes to the 1980 Summer Olympic Games in Moscow. Over 40 other countries also boycotted, or refused to participate in. As a result, only 80 countries participated—the lowest number since 1956.

John Lennon Murdered

On December 8, 1980, John Lennon, a musician and songwriter who had been a member of the world-renowned Beatles (see page 19), was entering his apartment building in New York City when a young man stepped out of the shadows. He shot the 40 year-old Lennon four times, killing him. The shooter, Mark David Chapman, was sentenced to 20 years in prison.

First U.S. Woman Travels in Space

When the space shuttle *Challenger* lifted off from Cape Kennedy Center in Florida on June 18, 1983, Sally Ride became the first U.S. woman to fly in space. She followed the first woman in space, Russia's Valentina Tereshkova, who had flown aboard *Vostok 6* in 1963.

Promises for the PC

In 1978 Melinda French was 14 years old, and a freshman at Ursuline Academy in Dallas, Texas. It was an all-girls high school. She was a good student who worked hard for her grades. She also volunteered at a hospital and tutored children at a public school. Like Bill Gates, Melinda had confidence in herself. She liked to set a goal each day, such as learning a new word or running a mile.

Melinda got hooked on computers in 1978. Her father brought home an Apple II computer to help run his business. The Apple II was one of the first computers that people bought for homes and schools. Melinda could not stay away from it. First, she helped her father with his business records. Then, she taught herself BASIC, the computer language. When her high school purchased Apple II computers, Melinda taught her teachers how to use them.[1]

GROWING MICROSOFT

When Melinda started high school, Bill Gates and Paul Allen were managing their small company, Microsoft. In 1978, 16 young, energetic employees worked there. Several were Gates's and Allen's friends from Lakeside School, including Richard Weiland. Gates expected them to work as hard as he did, and they came through for him. With his typical confidence, Gates promised computer companies that their software

Many people argue that the personal computer industry truly began in 1977, when Apple Computer, Inc. introduced the Apple II. This was one of the first fully assembled, mass-produced computers, and it set a new standard for affordability. The Apple II became very popular with schools in particular.

projects would be done in a few months. Then he and the programmers worked day and night to meet the deadlines.

Each software project required countless hours of programming, manual writing, and testing. These smart young programmers became known as Microkids. In the early days, they worked long hours simply because of their passion for computers. A few years later, Microsoft employees asked for and got overtime pay. Then that was replaced by pay bonuses based on the company's profits.[2]

"A computer on every desk and in every home"
—Microsoft motto

In 1979 Gates and Allen moved the company and almost all their employees back to Washington state. They moved into a bank building in Bellevue, a suburb of Seattle. Just for fun, they requested a special company phone number that ended in 8080. These last four digits were in honor of the microprocessor chip that brought them their success.[3]

ENTER STEVE BALLMER, AGAIN

In 1980 Gates wanted to hire someone to help him run the growing company. He called his Harvard friend Steve Ballmer, who was enrolled in Stanford Business School in California. Gates convinced Ballmer to move to Seattle and become Microsoft's business manager. Ballmer was in charge of the Microsoft employees. He also created plans for the company's profits.[4]

After three weeks, Gates and Ballmer had their first argument. Ballmer wanted to add 50 more employees to the Microsoft staff. Gates did not

IBM

In 1980 International Business Machines, or IBM, was one of the richest and most powerful companies in the United States. But the company has roots going back to 1896! The Tabulating Machine Company provided automatic punching and sorting machines to railway companies and to the U.S. Census Bureau. In 1911, The Tabulating Machine Company was sold and merged with three other companies to become CTR (Computing Tabulating Recording). The company changed its name to IBM in 1924. It quickly became the country's largest producer of time clocks and punch cards. Businesses used these to keep track of their employees' work hours, among other things. More advanced punch card systems were developed by IBM and proved extremely useful to governments implementing massive programs and keeping records of millions of people. There were also military applications for these machines. Starting in the 1950s, IBM became one of the first computer companies in the world.[5] It originally built computers only for the military and scientists, but as the technology continued to develop, the different uses for computers seemed endless.

want to take the risk. He was afraid the company would not make enough money to cover all the paychecks. Ballmer insisted the work could not get done without more people. Gates finally agreed—and it is a good thing he did![6]

A COMPUTER IN EVERY HOME

Gates and Allen dreamed that low-cost computers would one day be as common as telephones and television sets. The motto of Microsoft became "a computer on every desk and in every home."[7] They were a long way from their goal, but by the 1980s, people everywhere were buying personal computers. In 1980 Radio Shack had the most popular computer. It sold the TRS-80 for offices for about $8,000. Their scaled-down home unit sold for about $500. Apple Computer was in second place with its Apple II, priced at $1,000 to $3,000. All these computers had one thing in common: they used Microsoft BASIC software.[8]

IBM STEPS IN

From the 1960s to the 1980s, IBM (see box on page 47) was the leading manufacturer of mainframe computers. When other companies started making small computers, IBM did not join them. By the time IBM leaders decided that microcomputers might sell well, they had a lot of catching up to do.

In July of 1980, a representative of IBM contacted Bill Gates at Microsoft. He explained that IBM was designing its first microcomputer, though the project was top secret. IBM wanted Microsoft to provide the **operating system** and software. An operating system is the software that controls how the computer works. The operating system lets a person tell the computer what to do. It allows the hardware and software to work.

This was a huge opportunity for Microsoft. IBM was a big, successful business. If Microsoft could deliver the operating system and software for IBM, then Microsoft could also become a worldwide success.[9]

A SOLUTION

Could Microsoft meet IBM's demands? IBM wanted its personal computers in stores in less than a year. Microsoft employees were already working around the clock. Employees were doubling up in offices and sometimes sleeping there. The company would have to invest a lot of money to hire more people to work on the project. Even then, could they meet the tight deadline? If they failed to develop a good product, the Microsoft reputation—and IBM's—would suffer.[10]

Allen thought of a solution. He wanted to find an existing operating system and use it as a basis for Microsoft's new operating system.

This would make the project go faster. Gates contacted his friend Tim Paterson, a computer engineer at Seattle Computer Products. Paterson had made an operating system for that company. He called it QDOS, for "Quick and Dirty Operating System." ("Quick and dirty" is a phrase programmers use. It basically means, "Not perfect, but good enough!") Microsoft paid Seattle Computer for the rights to QDOS. Gates did not tell Seattle Computer that the operating system was for IBM, one of the most successful companies in the world.[11]

THE IBM DEAL

Gates, Ballmer, and a few other people from Microsoft flew to Florida to meet with IBM executives. Gates and Ballmer were excited and nervous to conduct business with such a traditional and powerful company. They looked very young, but wanted to appear as professional as possible. So, instead of their typical khaki pants and flannel shirts, they dressed in business suits. On the plane, Gates panicked. He forgot something important! On the way from the airport to the IBM offices, the Microsoft team stopped at a department store so Gates could buy a necktie.

The Microsoft and IBM people sat together for hours working on an agreement. The IBM executives questioned young Gates and Ballmer about their experience and skills. Then the young men made a bold demand. They wanted **royalty** payments for the software. Instead of IBM buying the software from Microsoft, IBM would pay Microsoft a portion of the money from the sale of every IBM computer that had Microsoft software. Gates was confident that IBM personal computers would be hugely successful and that Microsoft would ride the wave of success. IBM and Microsoft signed a contract on November 6, 1980.[12]

GETTING THE JOB DONE

IBM soon sent models of their secret personal computers (called PCs) to Seattle. They insisted that no one outside of the project see the computers or learn about the ongoing work. Gates and Ballmer put together a team to develop the operating system and software.

Microsoft had nine months to complete the project, with a series of intermediate deadlines to meet. IBM managers frequently dropped in to the Microsoft offices to check on the progress and be sure that the secret was still secure.[13]

In April 1981 Tim Paterson left Seattle Computer Products and went to work for Microsoft. He was going to refine his operating system for the PC. Eventually they started calling the operating system the PC-DOS. Later it was named **MS-DOS**, for "Microsoft Disk Operating System."[14]

"When you have a hot product, investors pay attention to you and are willing to put their money into your company. Smart kids think, 'Hey, everybody's talking about this company. I'd like to work there.'"
—Bill Gates

INTRODUCING THE PC

With MS-DOS and Microsoft software, IBM was ready to announce its PC (see box). On August 12, 1981, IBM invited reporters from newspapers, magazines, and television stations to an event in the ballroom at the Waldorf–Astoria Hotel in New York City. IBM distributed a press release that started:

> IBM Corporation today announced its smallest, lowest-priced computer system—the IBM Personal Computer. Designed for business, school, and home, the easy-to-use system sells for as little as $1,565. It offers many advanced features and, with optional software, may use hundreds of popular application programs.[15]

The IBM PC

The IBM PC offered state-of-the art features. First, it had amazing memory features. Memory in computers is measured in bytes. A byte can store one character. A kilobyte (K or KB) is about 1,000 bytes. (About one page of typewritten text takes up one kilobyte.) The IBM PC had 40K of built-in Read-Only Memory (ROM). ROM stays in the computer even after it is turned off. This memory has data that was prerecorded on the computer. ROM cannot be removed—it can only be read. The IBM PC also had 16K to 256K of Random-Access Memory (RAM), also called user memory. RAM holds the information that the user types in. If the user does not save this data, it will be lost when the computer is turned off.

In early microcomputers, people saved their data on cassette tapes. By the time the IBM PC came out, people used floppy disks. The IBM PC came with one or two floppy disk drives. It also came with an optional color monitor. For those who did not buy a monitor, they could hook up the computer to a television set. The PC also included several kinds of accounting software, along with **word-processing** software and a fantasy game called Microsoft Adventure.[16]

HERE COME THE CLONES!

The IBM PC was a huge success. Over the next four months, IBM sold more than 35,000 PCs. Microsoft earned money with each sale. By the end of 1982, Microsoft had earnings of $34 million. It had 200 employees.[17]

With all the buzz about the IBM PC, other computer companies began to copy it. These copies became known as clones. The competing companies wanted the MS-DOS operating system, and Microsoft was happy to sell it to them. According to the contract between Microsoft and

IBM, Microsoft could sell the operating system to anyone. It could also develop software for other companies.

Gates's company was on a wild ride of success. In his book *The Road Ahead*, Gates called this a "positive spiral." "When you have a hot product, investors pay attention to you and are willing to put their money into your company. Smart kids think, 'Hey, everybody's talking about this company. I'd like to work there.'" As Gates described it, many successful people wanted to be part of Microsoft—as employees, investors, and customers. This created more success![18]

A two-year-old girl poses with an early IBM PC, 1982.

WORD

Microsoft developed many kinds of software. In 1982 it introduced a spreadsheet program called Multiplan to keep track of finances for families and business. In 1983 it introduced a word-processing program called Word.

One thing was for sure: the personal computer was changing the way offices and families worked and played. In January 1983, *Time* magazine, which usually chose a "Person of the Year," gave the honor to the personal computer. The cover of the January 3, 1983, issue read: "Machine of the Year: The Computer Moves In."[19]

New technologies and music

The Walkman Debuts

In June 1979 the founder of the Sony Corporation in Japan, Akio Morita, announced a product "for all those young people who want to listen to music all day." Now people could take their favorite music with them on the Walkman TPS-L2. It was a battery-operated cassette player with dual earphones. The device took advantage of technology developed by Philips Electronics in 1963: the cassette tape.

World's First CD Produced

On August 17, 1982, a factory in Langenhagen, Germany, produced an invention that changed how people listen to music. The small, flat compact disk had several advantages over vinyl records and cassette tapes. The new CDs were more scratch resistant, more portable than vinyl, and had the potential to provide excellent sound quality. The invention was co-developed by Philips Corporation and Sony.

At a party in 1983, Gates met a computer sales representative named Jill Bennett. They began dating. It was his first serious relationship with a woman. Bennett explained in an interview that Gates's work left little time for a girlfriend. Gates boasted that he had a "seven-hour turnaround." When he left the office at night, he always returned seven hours later to start the next day. The couple broke up in 1984.[20]

PAUL ALLEN RESIGNS

In 1982 Paul Allen found out that he had cancer. Fortunately, he had radiation treatments and returned to good health. However, the experience changed his life's focus. In February 1983, Allen decided to resign from Microsoft (see box).[21]

Paul Allen after Microsoft

Thanks to Microsoft, Paul Allen became very rich. After he left Microsoft, he bought the Portland Trailblazers basketball team, the Seattle Seahawks football team, and became part owner of the Seattle Sounders soccer team. Like Gates, he gave millions of dollars to libraries, parks, museums, and medical research. In 1986 Gates and Allen donated $2.2 million to Lakeside School. The school built a science and math center. The building's auditorium was named after Kent Evans, the friend whom Gates and Allen lost in 1972.[22]

MELINDA FRENCH GOES TO COLLEGE

In 1982 Melinda French graduated from high school. She knew she wanted to study computer science in college. She graduated at the top of her class and could have attended almost any college. Melinda picked Duke University in North Carolina because it was expanding its computer science department.[23]

At Duke, Melinda had two majors: computer science and economics. She joined the freshmen advisory council and the Kappa Alpha Theta sorority. When high school students came to Duke, Melinda signed up to give campus tours. She dated a few young men in college, including William Wrigley, Jr., whose family owned the Wrigley gum company.[24]

A NEW GIRLFRIEND

Meanwhile, in 1984 Bill Gates began dating a woman named Ann Winblad. She had started a software company in Minneapolis, Minnesota, and sold it for $15 million. The couple met at a business conference. Winblad admired the fact that Gates was a risk taker. She also appreciated many of his quirks, such as bringing four magazines into a Burger King so he would not be bored while he waited. Though the two lived in different cities, they often had "virtual dates." They chose a movie and watched it at the same time. Then they discussed it on their cell phones. After dating for almost three years, Gates and Winblad broke up. They remained good friends.[25] ❖

Headlines from the Time of Microsoft's Rise to the Top: 1985–1993

Here are some major news stories from the time.

Shuttle *Challenger* Explodes After Liftoff

January 28, 1986: Little more than one minute after its liftoff from Cape Canaveral, Florida, the space shuttle *Challenger* exploded. The blast killed all seven crewmembers on board, including Christa McAuliffe, the first teacher ever chosen to fly on a shuttle mission. The deadly blast was shown live on television, shocking viewers around the world.

The O-ring seal on the Challenger's solid rocket booster failed, due to the cold temperature of the January morning. This caused flames to erupt, which caused damage to the shuttle's external fuel tank. Only 73 seconds after liftoff, the Challenger disappeared in a fiery cloud.

Explosion Rocks Chernobyl

Sixty-three minutes after midnight on April 26, 1986, an explosion rocked the Chernobyl nuclear power plant in the Soviet Union. A malfunctioning reactor blew the roof off the building and started numerous fires. Dangerous radioactive material filtered through the air. Nearly 300 people were treated for radiation poisoning. About 50 deaths were directly linked to the accident. However, thousands of deaths since the accident and in the future may be caused by the radioactive exposure.

The Berlin Wall Falls

Beginning in 1961, a 12-foot (4-meter) concrete wall divided the city of Berlin, Germany. It separated the communist country of East Germany from the democratic country of West Germany. Armed guards at the wall kept East German citizens from fleeing to West Germany. Then, in the 1980s, the Soviet Union started to become more open. Soviet leader Mikhail Gorbachev introduced a policy called *glasnost*. With it came more freedom of information and movement. By the summer of 1989, the East German government was weakening, and Hungary allowed East Germans to leave through its borders. On November 9, East German citizens began tearing down pieces of the wall, and no one stopped them. Eventually the East German government removed the wall and reunited with West Germany. Together they formed a nation called the Federal Republic of Germany.

Operation Desert Storm Begins

In 1990 Iraqi president Saddam Hussein invaded a neighboring country called Kuwait. U.S. President George H. W. Bush gathered a group of nations to work together to protect Kuwait's freedom, as well as the oil supply in Kuwait and Saudi Arabia. After Iraq failed to meet deadlines set by the United Nations, President Bush ordered air attacks on Iraq and Kuwait on January 16, 1991. On February 24, the coalition of the United States and other nations sent in ground troops and defeated the Iraqi army in four days. In a final act of destruction, Iraqi troops burned over 500 oil wells in Kuwait.

The Soviet Union Breaks Up

On December 25, 1991, Soviet President Mikhail Gorbachev resigned. The Soviet parliament dissolved the Soviet Union on December 26. The Soviet Union had been formed as a communist **dictatorship** in 1922. It was a union of states and republics stretching through eastern Europe and Asia. In size it was by far the largest country in the world. But by 1991 several of the republics took advantage of weaknesses in the Soviet government and the strengths within their own people. One by one, they declared their independence from the Soviet Union, leading to its final dissolution.

Friendlier Computers

In a commercial shown during the 1984 Super Bowl, Apple Computer, Inc., introduced its hot new computer, the Macintosh. It promised to change the way people used computers. And it did! An article in USA Today *said the "Mac," as it was called for short, "made computing simple for non-techies." It said that using a Mac compared to an MS-DOS computer was like the difference between writing a message with a ballpoint pen and writing it with a hammer and chisel.*[1]

The Mac had a new "user-friendly" operating system called a **graphic user interface**, or GUI. Computer buffs called it "gooey." While PC users had to type a long list of commands, Mac users held an attachment called a mouse. They simply pointed to symbols on the computer screen and clicked the mouse.[2]

Since 1982 Gates had worked with the head of Apple, Steve Jobs, to develop Macintosh software. Microsoft developed two popular software programs for it: a financial spreadsheet program called Excel and a word-processing program called Word.

Gates loved the mouse technology that Apple was using. He wanted Microsoft to make similar software for the IBM PC and other personal computers. Microsoft programmers created a new operating system called Windows. It made the PC screens look similar to the Mac's.[3] Windows became very successful. However, it also made enemies for Microsoft. Apple went to court and accused Microsoft of stealing features from the Macintosh. The court ruled that Microsoft could continue with Windows. This was a big victory for Gates. Eventually most PCs came with a package of Windows software.[4]

GETTING FAMOUS

By 1983 Bill Gates was famous. National magazines such as the *Wall Street Journal*, *People*, and *Fortune* sent reporters to interview him. Some were surprised to find out that Microsoft's 28-year-old leader looked like a skinny teenager with uncombed hair and oversized glasses. The *Wall Street Journal* called him a "nerd." *People* magazine named him one of "The 25 Most Intriguing People" of 1983. They compared him to Thomas Edison, the inventor of the lightbulb. *People* called Gates "part innovator, part entrepreneur, part salesman, and full-time genius."[5]

On April 16, 1984, Gates was on the cover of *Time* magazine. The article called him "The Wizard Inside the Machine." There were at least 1,000 companies making software, but Microsoft was the largest. It was bringing in about $100 million a year.[6]

No one could deny that Gates ran a successful business. But what was he like as a boss? Employees reported that he was never afraid of a challenge or an argument. He fired out questions and expected quick

The Nintendo Entertainment System

The Nintendo Corporation introduced its Nintendo Entertainment System in 1985, and it became an instant hit with its lineup of home video games. Games such as *Super Mario Brothers*, *Duck Hunt*, and *The Legend of Zelda* were instant hits.

answers. He was famous for telling people that their ideas were "the stupidest thing I've ever heard." Most employees were proud to report that Gates had directed his famous line to them![7]

ANOTHER MOVE

By 1986 Microsoft had over 1,000 employees. It was time to move to new offices. This time Gates said in an interview that he wanted to work in "a fun environment, a lot like a college campus." He found land in a wooded area in nearby Redmond, Washington. He had several buildings, walking paths, volleyball nets, a basketball court, and a soccer field built. The inside of the offices resembled college dorm rooms. Young employees covered their desks and bookcases with stacks of pizza boxes and empty soda cans.[8]

"If you wanted to figure out how many times on average you would have to flip the pages of the Manhattan phone book to find a specific name, how would you approach the problem?"
—Microsoft job interview question

When hiring new people, Gates and the other top managers looked for smart young people, but not necessarily those with a lot of work experience. When they interviewed applicants, they cared less about what a person knew and more about how the person thought. For example, they asked: "If you wanted to figure out how many times on average you would have to flip the pages of the Manhattan phone book to find a specific name, how would you approach the problem?"[9]

MICROSOFT GOES PUBLIC

In the early 1980s, Microsoft employees were rewarded with valuable shares of Microsoft **stock**. When people own stock in a company, they own a portion of the company. If the company makes money, **shareholders** earn money. If the company loses money, the shareholders also lose. As Microsoft succeeded, many employees became very wealthy after they sold their Microsoft stock.[10]

On March 13, 1986, Microsoft started to sell shares of stock to the public. This would help raise more money for the company's growth. This first public offering raised $61 million for Microsoft. Gates owned 45 percent of the company, at a value of $350 million. He became a multimillionaire at the age of 30. On the first morning of trading Microsoft stock, a share cost $21. One year later, the price was $90 a share. Gates then became the youngest billionaire in the United States.[11]

MELINDA FRENCH JOINS MICROSOFT

One of the many new employees at Microsoft in 1987 was 22-year-old Melinda French. She had received a bachelor's degree in computer science and economics and then a master's degree in business

Not just software

Since 1986 Microsoft has branched into other areas of business, including:

- 1989: Corbis Corporation, a collection of photographs and film footage

- 1990: *Encarta*, an online encyclopedia

- 1995: Explorer, an Internet **browser**

- 1996: MSNBC, a cable news system

- 2002: Xbox, a games system[12]

The Microsoft Corporation Campus in Redmond, Washington. Bill Gates moved his company to this new location on February 26, 1986.

administration from Duke. During one of her college summers, Melinda worked for IBM. During her senior year, people from Microsoft went to Duke to interview students for jobs. Melinda French was hired.[13]

Melinda moved to Seattle from her home in Dallas. Her first role was as marketing manager of word-processing software. Melinda became known as a good manager because she encouraged teamwork. Eventually she had 300 employees working on her teams.

When she first came to Microsoft, she thought it was a tense place to work. Managers seemed demanding, typically barking orders at their staff. She heard that this gruff behavior trickled down from the company executives—particularly the CEO, Bill Gates.[14]

FUNNIER THAN EXPECTED

Four months after Melinda began her job, she and Bill Gates traveled to New York City for the same business event. At a group dinner, she met him for the first time. Her first impression was, "He certainly was funnier than I expected him to be."

One Saturday afternoon after returning from New York, Bill and Melinda ran into each other again in a Microsoft parking lot. Bill asked, "Will you go out with me two weeks from Friday night?" Melinda replied that she did not make plans that far ahead. Bill was determined to get a date. When he got home that night, he called Melinda. They agreed to go out that very evening.[15]

Melinda was hesitant to date the head of the company. She was proud of the career she was building at Microsoft. She did not want anyone to think she was getting promoted because she was dating the CEO. But she and Bill enjoyed their time together. They had much in common. They both read lots of books and loved computers. In addition, they both enjoyed tackling complicated jigsaw puzzles and talking about hundreds of things. So they dated quietly. She refused to attend any business events with him. When reporters finally learned that Bill Gates was seriously dating someone, Bill asked them not to report her name, and they respected his wishes.[16]

SUCCESS IN A MAN'S WORLD

Over the course of her nine years at Microsoft, Melinda was very successful. She was the general manager of products that included Expedia travel services and the *Encarta* online encyclopedia.[17]

Melinda had a career in computers at a time when mostly men worked in the field. She often talked about a high school math teacher who was her role model. The teacher had encouraged the school to buy computers and had urged the female students to learn computer programming. In a 1997 speech, Melinda encouraged members of the audience to buy computers for girls. She urged people to give girls a boost into a job market that now required computer skills.[18]

Melinda French and Bill Gates during their engagement, Seattle, Washington.

WEDDING PLANS

In 1993 Bill Gates and Melinda French got engaged. On Easter Sunday, they were flying home on a private plane from a visit with Bill's parents in Palm Springs, California. Bill secretly asked the pilot to stop in Omaha, Nebraska, where his friend Warren Buffett (see box) owned a jewelry store. Buffett opened the store for them, and they picked out an engagement ring.[19]

"While I understand that your readers may find my story interesting because of the man I married, it is a personal decision for me not to share information about our relationship or my personal life with the world at large."
—Melinda Gates, talking about why she keeps her personal life private

Melinda's life was changing course. It was a course she never could have predicted. Now she would be married to a billionaire who was the CEO of the company where she worked. She told her coworkers and bosses that she wanted no special treatment. In the company cafeteria, she stood in line with everyone else.[20]

Bill was used to the reporters and security guards who followed him ever since his wealth became public. Melinda, however, did not wish to be a public figure.

After her wedding, she answered an interview request from a Seattle reporter by saying, "While I understand that your readers may find my story interesting because of the man I married, it is a personal decision for me not to share information about our relationship or my personal life with the world at large."[21] ❖

Warren Buffett

Bill Gates met Warren Buffett at a dinner in 1991. A mutual friend, Katharine Graham (head of the *Washington Post* newspaper), thought they should meet. After all, they were both among the richest people in the world. Gates didn't want to go. He flew in on a helicopter so he could leave quickly. However, once he and Buffett met, they found endless things to talk about. Buffett did not even own a computer, but Gates talked him into buying one. They stayed good friends from then on.[22]

HEADLINES FROM THE FIRST YEARS OF MARRIAGE: 1994–2001

Here are some major news stories from the time.

Golf's Youngest Champ Wins Masters

On April 13, 1997, at the age of 21, Eldrick (Tiger) Woods became the youngest person to win the famous Masters golf tournament. Woods began playing golf almost as soon as he started walking. As a child, he appeared on television shows, showing off his awesome skill. By the age of six, he had twice shot a hole in one. After winning teen and college tournaments, Woods turned professional. At the 1997 Masters Tournament, he set records for youngest champion, lowest score for 72 holes, and widest margin of victory. He also became the first African American and the first Asian American golfer to win the Masters.

Harry Potter Arrives

Readers in the U.K. met a young wizard named Harry Potter in June 1997, with the publication of *Harry Potter and the Philosopher's Stone*. The book was published in the United States in September 1998 as *Harry Potter and the Sorcerer's Stone*. The author, Joanne Kathleen (J. K.) Rowling, began writing the book on a train from Manchester to London, England.

Terrorists Attack the United States

Early on a clear Tuesday morning, on September 11, 2001, hijackers crashed two planes into the Twin Towers of the World Trade Center in New York City. Minutes later, another hijacked plane crashed into the Pentagon building in Washington, D.C. Passengers on a fourth plane overpowered their hijackers, who were heading for other Washington buildings. That plane crashed in Shanksville, Pennsylvania. After they were hit, the World Trade Center buildings collapsed. Nearly 3,000 people died that day, including the airline passengers, people in the buildings, firefighters, police, and the 19 hijackers. The hijackers were identified as Islamic radicals from a terrorist group called al Qaeda.

The first hijacked plane crashed into the north tower of the World Trade Center before 9:00 a.m. The south tower was struck by a second plane 17 minutes later. After the crashes, massive amounts of jet fuel burned at extremely high temperatures, eventually melting through steel supports and causing both towers to collapse. The south tower collapsed first, the north followed about 30 minutes later.

A Life Together

Bill Gates, at age 38, and Melinda French, at age 29, got married on January 1, 1994. No reporters were allowed at the wedding. Bill and Melinda rented the entire Manele Bay Hotel resort on the beautiful Hawaiian island of Lanai. The ceremony was held on the golf course. Throughout the day security guards patrolled the course in golf carts, looking for photographers or suspicious characters. Before the ceremony, Paul Allen treated the wedding guests to a champagne brunch on his 154-foot (47-meter) yacht.

As the sun began to set, a stream of golf carts brought the 130 guests to a gathering place at the tee box of the 12th hole. The scene was breathtaking, with a rugged cliff dropping 150 feet (50 meters) to the Pacific Ocean. Bill stood with his best man, Steve Ballmer. Gates wore a white jacket and black pants. Ballmer wore a tuxedo. Bill's parents sat in the first row. His mother, Mary, was seriously ill with cancer and was thrilled to finally see her son get married. Five bridesmaids wearing pink dresses marched down the aisle. Then came Melinda, wearing a traditional white wedding dress. After the wedding, a spokesperson made a simple statement for the couple: "We are both extremely happy and looking forward to a long, wonderful life together."[1]

Newlyweds Bill and Melinda Gates greet guests at a reception in Seattle, one week after they were married in Hawaii.

In the first years of their marriage, Melinda and Bill worked long hours at Microsoft. Melinda had always enjoyed rigorous exercise. She continued to run daily. She had run in the Seattle Marathon and climbed to the peak of Mount Rainer in Washington. Bill took up golf after the wedding, and he treated it as he did his other projects—addictively and competitively. Together Bill and Melinda enjoyed taking walks and playing tennis and golf.[2]

DREAM HOUSE

Bill Gates started planning his dream house before he met Melinda. He chose to place it in a wooded area overlooking Lake Washington. It is located in Medina, near Seattle. After Bill and Melinda married, she added her ideas to the plans. She wanted to make the house better suited to a family. As with all his projects, Bill painstakingly designed every detail of the house. The house is perfect for this electronics wizard and billionaire.[3]

HIGH-TECH HOME

Bill and Melinda's house has cozy, small rooms for one or two people to watch television and read. It also has large rooms, like the one that can seat 100 people for dinner. There is a movie theater, a library with two secret bookcase doors, a 60-foot (18-meter) pool with an underwater music system, and a domed trampoline room. Outside there are several sports courts near the water and a dock for one of Bill's favorite sports, waterskiing. The underground garage can hold 30 cars.[4]

Guests receive a pin when they enter the front door. The pin is electronically connected to the home's lighting, music, and art systems. The electronics system is programmed with the favorite music and artwork of the guests. First-time guests make their choices when they enter the house. The choices are stored and replayed when a guest returns. As a guest enters a room, the lights go on and his or her favorite music fills the room. Lights and music fade as the person leaves. Guests

Bill and Melinda Gates's home in Medina, Washington.

can choose from thousands of art images, movies, and television shows that appear on the screens in the room. If two people enter a room together, the system can be programmed to select something that both people like.[5]

In addition to the electronic art images, Bill and Melinda started buying original art in the 1990s. They have a painting by Winslow Homer for which they may have spent the highest price ever paid for a U.S. painting—$36 million. One of Bill's most prized possessions is a scientific notebook that belonged to Italian artist Leonardo da Vinci in the early 1500s. Bill bought it in 1994 for $30.8 million.[6]

THE GATES CHILDREN

In 1996 Bill and Melinda's first child, Jennifer, was born. That year, Melinda decided to leave Microsoft to be home with Jennifer. In 1999 their son, Rory, was born. Their younger daughter, Phoebe, was born in 2002.

In 1997 Bill, Melinda, and Jennifer moved into their new, unfinished house. While Bill's life was very public, Melinda wanted their family life to be private and normal. On the weekends, Melinda sent home all of the household staff except for the security guards and sometimes a babysitter who watched the children if she and Bill went out for dinner. Wednesday night became family swimming night. Friday night was family movie night. Like their parents, the children learned to enjoy reading books, playing games, and finishing 1,000-piece jigsaw puzzles. When the family walked in the community or went out to restaurants, neighbors respected their privacy.[7]

Waiting for Y2K

As the year 2000 approached, the world tried to prepare for an unknown computer crisis. Computers were set to read the last two digits of a year, such as 99 for 1999. Without adjustment, the computers would read the year 2000 as 1900. Some predicted disastrous computer crashes everywhere, from banks and gas stations to airlines, telephone systems, and traffic signals. Computer programmers and engineers spent 1999 making adjustments to avoid Y2K problems. When the clock struck midnight on December 31, 1999, the computer problems were minimal.

Are the Gates children always at their computers? Definitely not, says Bill. When Jennifer turned 10, she was an avid computer game player. Bill and Melinda noticed that she spent two or three hours a day on one game. They decided to limit computer-game time to 45 minutes a day during the week and an hour on weekend days. Additional computer time was permitted for schoolwork. When their son, Rory, was told about this rule, he asked, "Am I going to have limits like this my whole life?" Bill answered, only half-jokingly, "No, when you move away, you can set your own screen limits."[8]

"They need to know the problems in this world and their own responsibility in addressing them. They need to know that they should give back."
—Melinda Gates, talking about how she raises her children

GOOD LESSONS

Bill remembers the lessons about money that his parents taught him. He wants to pass those along to his own children. They each get an allowance and learn that there are limits to what they can buy.[9]

Bill and Melinda want their children to learn the message that Bill's mother gave to him: From those to whom much is given, much is expected. When Melinda was in India in 2004, she told a reporter how she shares her concerns about the world with her children. "When I come out on visits such as these, I go back and talk to them," she said. "They need to know the problems in this world and their own responsibility in addressing them. They need to know that they should give back."[10]

GIVING BACK

By the early 1990s, Bill Gates was one of the wealthiest people in the world. Many charities asked him for money. Bill wanted to use his money for good causes, but he thought he would wait until he finished his career at Microsoft, at about age 65. Some people criticized him for not helping others right away. Bill's father, Bill Sr., encouraged Bill and Melinda to start a foundation. He offered to help. In 1994 they started the William H. Gates Foundation. Bill Sr. set up an office in his basement. He went through piles of mail and made suggestions to Bill for donating money. The foundation donated $2 million to the Seattle Area YMCA, $20 million to the Seattle Public Library, and $1 million to the Tacoma Art Museum. The foundation also gave money to educational programs and global health causes.[11]

"All lives have equal value."
—statement on the Gates Foundation website

Melinda had volunteered in schools where students were failing and dropping out. She thought about the advantages students in wealthier neighborhoods had. In particular, they had computers and technology. She believed in a statement that runs across the top of the Gates Foundation website: "All lives have equal value."[12]

GATES LEARNING FOUNDATION

In 1997 Bill and Melinda started another foundation, the Gates Library Foundation. As Bill Sr. explained in a 2004 speech: "Knowledge cannot come without information; and information—for many of our citizens—cannot come without libraries. Libraries allow citizens to borrow what they can't afford to buy." The Gates Library Foundation provided more than 22,000 computers in about 4,500 libraries in the United States, and 4,000 computers in Canadian libraries.[13]

"Libraries allow citizens to borrow what they can't afford to buy."
—Bill Gates Senior

In February 1999 the Gates Library Foundation changed its name to the Gates Learning Foundation. The foundation promised to give $1 billion to provide college scholarships to 20,000 minority students over the next 20 years. In 2000 a similar scholarship program was created to send students from **developing countries** to graduate school at the University of Cambridge, in England. In 2000 the different Gates foundations were merged into one: The Bill and Melinda Gates Foundation. By 2007 it would be giving out over $2 billion a year.[14]

THE INTERNET TAKES OFF

As Bill Gates's personal life changed, so did his professional life. By the 1990s, millions of people had desktop computers. These computers changed the way offices did business, doctors kept medical records, travelers picked destinations, and children did homework. Throughout the 1990s, computers became even more crucial as the Internet revolution swept through the world (see box on page 76). The Internet instantly connected people to information, places, and one another. In his book *The Road Ahead*, Gates described how the Internet can allow people to "call up great entertainment, make friends, go to neighborly markets, and show pictures to your relatives, wherever they are—without leaving your desk or your armchair."[15]

NETSCAPE

In the early 1990s, a company called Netscape created an extremely popular web browser, which is a program people use to find information on the Internet. Netscape was far and away the most successful of these browsers. It was easy to use and pages were displayed on screen more quickly than other browsers. The speed at which pages could be read was key. In these days, the connection speeds were much slower than they are now, so it could take several minutes for a page to load completely. The Netscape browser displayed information as it loaded. So text could typically be read right away. The pictures and graphics would follow. Netscape also developed and offered frequent updates to its browser. This was important to the company's success, because the speed at which the Internet changed and advanced quickly made older browsers obsolete.

Microsoft did not jump into the Internet market as early as other software companies. Gates and his team did not expect the Internet to become popular as quickly as it did. They expected that it would take years before online services could overcome the problems of slowness, privacy,

The Internet

The Internet is sometimes called the "information superhighway." It is a system of interconnected computer networks. The Internet grew out of a U.S. government communications network from the 1960s, called ARPANET. In the 1970s and 1980s, the government funded this network, which was used for military and academic purposes. In the 1990s the Internet's World Wide Web became popular for e-mails, search engines, chat rooms, bulletin boards, and blogs.[16]

> *"People complained about the Internet's irritating deficiencies, but that didn't stop them from using this exciting new way to communicate. It was too much fun to ignore."*
> —Bill Gates, talking about the rise of the Internet

security, and reliability. They thought most people would not bother with the Internet until these problems were solved. They were very wrong. As Gates said in his book: "Seemingly overnight, people by the millions went onto the Internet, demonstrating that they would endure a lot more in the way of shortcomings than we had expected. People complained about the Internet's irritating deficiencies, but that didn't stop them from using this exciting new way to communicate. It was too much fun to ignore."[17]

MICROSOFT UNFAIR?

By 1995 Microsoft had developed a browser called Explorer. Now Gates was ready to fiercely compete with Netscape. It is said that Gates went to computer manufacturers and strong-armed them into putting Explorer on all their personal computers. If a manufacturer wanted to put Netscape or another browser on its machine, Microsoft threatened to cancel its software license. According to one expert, in 2003, more than 95 percent of people who surfed the web used Internet Explorer.[18]

Many people said that Microsoft's business practices were unfair. There were several browsers on the market, but customers did not have a choice because their computers came with Explorer. In 1998 the U.S. government and 20 states joined together to file a lawsuit against Microsoft. They accused Microsoft of being an illegal monopoly. A monopoly has complete control over a product or service. When a company has a **monopoly**, other companies have trouble staying in business. According to the case, Microsoft's practices prevented other software companies from fairly getting business.[19]

LEGAL ISSUES

Gates spent many months in Washington, D.C., answering questions before Judge Thomas Penfield Jackson. In 2000 the judge declared that Microsoft was guilty of unfair business practices. He ordered Microsoft to split into two companies. This would make it less powerful and allow smaller companies a better chance to compete.[20]

Microsoft took the case to an **appeals court** to try to get a new decision. Gates insisted that Microsoft needed to be one large company. Its large size allowed it to continue to come up with new ideas for its customers.

Attack of the Love Bug

On May 4, 2000, millions of people opened an e-mail message with the subject line "ILOVEYOU." The message seemed to come from someone known to the user. When opened, however, the message released a computer **virus** that destroyed files, accessed login names and passwords, and sent them back to the creator of the virus. Authorities estimated that this "Love Bug" caused between $7 and $10 billion in damages to businesses and individuals. Police traced the virus to a computer in an apartment in Manila, in the Philippines. The alleged creators of the virus were detained during the investigation, but the charges against them were eventually dropped.

On June 28, 2001, Judge Colleen Kollar-Kotelly from the appeals court ruled that Judge Jackson's decision was too harsh. She suggested that Microsoft and the government try to work out a settlement. On November 2, 2001, the two sides reached an agreement.

Microsoft did not have to split into two companies. It did, however, have to make some changes. For example, Microsoft could not stop computer-makers from putting competing software on their computers. Microsoft's legal issues did not end, however. Several states and even the European Union continued to question Microsoft's power.[21] ❖

HEADLINES FROM THE GATES'S TRANSITIONAL YEARS: 2002–PRESENT

Here are some major news stories from the time.

War Begins in Iraq

In the period after the September 11, 2001, terrorist attacks, U.S. President George W. Bush spoke out against Iraqi President Saddam Hussein's alleged weapons of mass destruction and links to terrorism. On March 20, 2003, U.S. and British forces, along with small units from Poland and Australia, hit Iraq with air strikes. U.S. troops took over Iraq's capital of Baghdad within three weeks. However, a guerilla war continued for several years and brought thousands of deaths. About 16 countries joined the U.S. military and security forces in Iraq. It was later found that there were no weapons of mass destruction.

Tsunami Hits Indian Ocean

On December 26, 2004, a massive earthquake in the Indian Ocean caused the worst tsunami disaster in history. The giant wave, called a tsunami, hit the coasts of 14 countries from Southeast Asia to northeastern Africa. More than 250,000 people died.

Hurricane Katrina

On August 29, 2005, Hurricane Katrina ripped through the U.S. Gulf Coast, destroying towns in Alabama, Mississippi, and Louisiana. The storm overwhelmed structures called levees, which were holding back water from the city of New Orleans. When the levees broke, 80 percent of New Orleans was underwater. While most people escaped the city before the destruction hit, about 100,000 were left with no electricity, food, or drinking water. About 20,000 made their way to an emergency shelter in a sports stadium called the Superdome, only to find the sweltering, crowded conditions totally inadequate.

Barack Obama Becomes President

On January 20, 2009, Barack Obama became the first African American president of the United States. Obama was a young senator from Illinois when he decided to run as the Democratic candidate for president. At the time, many U.S. citizens had strong concerns about the war in Iraq, the country's economic challenges, dependence on foreign oil, and inaccessible health care. Obama promised to bring change to the country. His campaign set up offices in all 50 states and reached out to Americans through the Internet. He raised an unprecedented $750 million for his campaign, much of it through small donations of $100 or less. The election had the highest voter turnout since 1968.

A Major Shift

Even after the trial, criticism followed Bill Gates. Yet he kept working to drive Microsoft products forward. His workdays continued to be long and busy. At his desk, his eyes and hands shifted between two computers. One had four frames of text and data. The other displayed his hundreds of e-mail messages and memos. Two weeks every year, he stepped away from the daily business to have his "think weeks." He tried to ignore e-mails, meetings, and memos and instead only read and thought about the future.[1]

He also spent time at the Seattle headquarters of the Bill and Melinda Gates Foundation. He approached the foundation's goals much as he did Microsoft's. When he identified a problem, he went after the best possible solution. He did not accept excuses.[2]

A ROLE MODEL

Melinda Gates's life was busy, too. She worked hard to balance being a mom and working for the foundation. As the Gates children grew, she spent time helping at their school. At night, she often hosted guests of the foundation for dinner.

Melinda valued her privacy and would have liked to stay out of the public view. However, over time, she has agreed to speak in front of groups and give interviews. One reason she did this was to set an example for her daughters. When her older daughter, Jennifer, was 11, Melinda wanted to encourage her to voice her own opinions. In 2008 Melinda told *Fortune*, a business magazine, "I really want her to have a voice, whatever she chooses to do. I need to role-model that for her."[3]

"I really want her to have a voice, whatever she chooses to do. I need to role-model that for her."
—Melinda Gates, on her daughter Jennifer

"WE LIKE DIFFICULT"

In a 2008 interview, Melinda told a funny story that made her think her role-modeling was working. She walked past the bedroom of her youngest daughter, Phoebe, and saw the two-year-old struggling to tie her shoe. As Phoebe grappled with the shoelaces, she groaned, "This is difficult." Then she surprised her mother by saying, "I *like* difficult." Melinda told the interviewer, "For about a year, our motto at the foundation was 'We like difficult.'"[4]

Melinda sometimes gives speeches to groups that support the foundation's health and education projects. She admits that she gets nervous before she speaks to large groups of people. But she still manages to speak to groups, such as Powerful Voices (an organization that helps adolescent girls gain confidence), the Gates Foundation Malaria Forum (a group of doctors, scientists, and health officials that have joined to fight this disease), and the Fortune Most Powerful Women Summit (a gathering of successful female leaders of business, government, and the arts).[5]

LEARNING TOURS

At least once a year, Melinda and Bill travel around the globe to towns and villages where people are suffering the most. Sometimes they bring their children with them. Bill and Melinda call these trips "learning tours." They meet people, visit hospitals, talk to doctors, and try to find ways to help.

Bill and Melinda prepare for these trips by reading about problems and what the researchers are doing. Their offices are side-by-side at the foundation. Bill may read an article and put it on Melinda's desk. She will read others and pass them on to Bill. They talk about the articles for hours, often while they are taking long walks near home.[6]

GLOBAL HEALTH PROBLEMS

In a speech for the Seattle Biomedical Research Institute's Global Health Celebration in 2008, Melinda described how she and Bill got interested in global health problems. They had read a news article that said 500,000 children in poor countries were dying each year from a disease called **rotavirus**. "Imagine everybody in Seattle dying," she told her audience. She shared the article with Bill. They started to read about rotavirus and learned that it barely exists in the United States. In economically **developed countries**, children can be given products called rehydration fluids to combat the diarrhea caused by rotavirus. These products never reached the poorer countries. "The world knew how to treat those children," she said. "They just didn't do it."[7]

---

*"The world knew how to treat those children…
They just didn't do it."*
—Melinda Gates, on children in poor countries
who had died from curable diseases

The same is true of other diseases such as polio, tetanus, diphtheria, and measles. Doctors can prevent these diseases with **vaccines**. A vaccine is a drug that keeps the body from getting a disease. The foundation has saved hundreds of thousands of lives in poorer countries by sending vaccines and medicine to them.[8]

On a recent trip to Africa, Bill and Melinda found that the sexually-transmitted disease HIV is a huge problem. In some African countries, such as Botswana and Swaziland, as much as 20 percent of the adult population is infected with the disease. Bill and Melinda are currently helping to develop a product that the woman can use to protect herself from catching the virus and developing AIDS.

Bill and Melinda learn many lessons on their trips. In April 2007 they traveled to Vietnam, a country that was successfully giving vaccines to its children. The foundation was sending a new vaccine to this region, and it would soon arrive in large containers. On their visit, Bill and Melinda noticed that health care workers stored their medicine in small refrigerators, which were already full. They saw that the new vaccine would never fit in these small, full refrigerators. They quickly realized that two things were needed. The foundation went back to the drug manufacturer and asked it to repackage the vaccine in smaller containers. Then they put the word out to researchers that someone needed to develop vaccines that do not need refrigeration.[9]

SUPPORTING NEW IDEAS

The Gates Foundation supports research for new ideas. For example, it awards $100,000 to the winner of the Grand Challenges Exploration contest, which encourages scientists to solve global health problems. One award was given to a Japanese researcher who was trying to see if mosquitoes can inject vaccines as they bite humans.[11]

Of the approximately $2 billion the Gates Foundation gives away each year, much of this is Bill and Melinda Gates's own money. The foundation also receives contributions from other people and organizations that believe in its work. Bill's good friend Warren Buffett is one of these contributors.[12]

A GENEROUS DONATION

Bill Gates and Warren Buffett have been good friends for many years. Since they met in 1991 (see page 65), they have enjoyed discussing business, playing cards, and vacationing with their families. Gates is on the board of directors of Buffett's Berkshire Hathaway company. Likewise, Buffett is a trustee of the Gates Foundation. Buffett is one of the few people Gates turns to for advice. Buffett also shares Gates's strong desire to help others with his money. In 2006 Buffett announced that he would give away an astounding 85 percent of his wealth to charity. Most of it would go to the Bill and Melinda Gates Foundation. In 2006 the value of his contribution was about $1.5 billion.[13]

Forbes, a business magazine, tracks the wealth of the world's billionaires through the years. Beginning in 1995, Bill Gates was the wealthiest billionaire. In 2008 Warren Buffett took over the number-one spot. In fact, that year, Gates, worth $58 billion, was third. The second-richest man was Carlos Slim Helú, who controls more than 90 percent of Mexico's phone industry. As the value of their investments go up and down, it is likely that these men—and eventually other people as well— will exchange places on the *Forbes* list in the future.[14]

"Starting two years from now, I will . . .
work full-time at the foundation,
[and only] part time at Microsoft."
—Bill Gates in 2006, announcing
his plans for the future

GATES STEPS DOWN

On June 15, 2006, employees and reporters filled a large room at Microsoft. Bill Gates stood at a podium in front of the crowd. Steve Ballmer, his friend and Microsoft's CEO, stood beside him. Cameras clicked away, sending the images from the room over a webcast to employees in other Microsoft offices around the world. Gates began to speak:

> I'd like to share with you today some significant news concerning my personal plans and the plans of the company. . . . Starting two years from now, I will . . . work full-time at the foundation, [and only] part time at Microsoft.[15]

Gates recalled how he and Paul Allen had started Microsoft 30 years before:

> We had big dreams about software. . . . I never imagined what an incredible and important company would spring from those original ideas. I have one of the best jobs in the world.[16]

Gates wanted to stay at Microsoft two more years, so that there would be a smooth change of leadership. Ballmer would continue as CEO. Gates would continue to be chairman of the board of directors as well as senior technical advisor. He would also continue to be the largest shareholder of stocks.[17]

Two years passed, and in July 2008 Gates and Ballmer once again stood in front of a crowd at the Microsoft headquarters. Gates wiped tears from his face as the crowd applauded him. He said:

> There won't be a day of my life that I'm not thinking about Microsoft and the great things that it's doing, and wanting to help. So thank you for making it the center of my life, and so much fun.[18]

GIVING IT AWAY

Bill Gates now spends most of his time at the foundation office.

> *"A very rich person should leave his kids enough to do anything, but not enough to do nothing."*
> —Billionaire Warren Buffett, discussing his plans to leave most of his money to charity rather than to his children

Though he is not at Microsoft every day, his thoughts often drift there. He reported that sometimes when he is driving his kids to school, he automatically heads toward the office instead. They shout, "Dad, Dad, what are you going to do at Microsoft?"[19]

Jennifer, Rory, and Phoebe Gates will learn many valuable lessons from their parents. They will learn about working hard and about giving to others. Bill and Melinda plan to give away 95 percent of their wealth to charity instead of passing it all on to their children. They agree with their

Philanthropy

A philanthropist is someone who gives money or time to a charitable cause or causes. Anyone who volunteers some or donates just a little amount of money is engaging in philanthropy, but the term is most often used to describe very wealthy people and organizations who do charitable work with their money. Philanthropic causes can be anything from helping to end world hunger, fighting disease, and stopping animal cruelty to donating money to an educational institution or museum.

friend Warren Buffett, who said, "A very rich person should leave his kids enough to do anything, but not enough to do nothing." Like Buffett's children, Jennifer, Rory, and Phoebe may run foundations of their own when they grow up.[20]

CREATING CHANGE

Bill and Melinda Gates want to make the world a better place through their foundation. They have received many awards for their generous work. In 2005 *Time* magazine named them (along with U2 lead singer Bono) its "Persons of the Year." The same year, Queen Elizabeth II of Great Britain presented Bill with an honorary knighthood for being "one of the most important business leaders of his age." In 2006 Bill received the James C. Morgan Global Humanitarian Award, which works to honor people who address the world's biggest problems. In 2007 the Save the Children organization honored Melinda for her efforts in saving the lives of newborn babies around the world. For several years *Forbes* magazine named Melinda one of their "100 Most Powerful Women."[21]

A HARVARD DEGREE... FINALLY!

In June 2007 Harvard University awarded Bill an honorary degree. Since Bill never graduated from college, this was an especially exciting moment for him. After taking his diploma, he spoke to the graduating class. First, he joked, saying, "I've been waiting more than 30 years to say this: 'Dad, I always told you I'd come back and get my degree.'"[22]

"Be activists. Take on the big inequities [injustices]. It will be one of the great experiences of your lives."
—Bill Gates, giving advice to young people

Then he gave an inspiring speech to the Harvard students. He encouraged them to pick a complex world problem and learn everything about it. He urged them to use the power of the Internet to gather information and to meet other people interested in the same issues. He said:

> You graduates are coming of age in an amazing time. As you leave Harvard, you have technology that members of my class never had. You have awareness of global inequity [injustices], which we did not have. And with that awareness, you likely also have an informed conscience that will torment you if you abandon these people whose lives you could change with very little effort. You have more than we had; you must start sooner, and carry on longer. Knowing what you know, how could you not?

At the end of his inspiring speech, Bill concluded, "Be activists. Take on the big inequities. It will be one of the great experiences of your lives."[23]

Bill Gates should know. He and Melinda Gates have taken on many complex problems and made great experiences out of them. Their efforts have changed the world. ❖

Timeline

1955   William H. Gates III is born on October 28.

1961   YURI GAGARIN, A RUSSIAN ASTRONAUT, BECOMES THE FIRST HUMAN TO BE LAUNCHED INTO SPACE.

1962   THE UNITED STATES AND SOVIET UNION ENGAGE IN A STANDOFF OVER NUCLEAR MISSILES. IT IS KNOWN AS THE CUBAN MISSILE CRISIS.

        THERE ARE 10,000 COMPUTERS IN THE WORLD. THEY ARE EXPENSIVE AND HUGE.

        A BRANCH OF THE U.S. DEPARTMENT OF DEFENSE BEGINS WORK ON ARPANET, WHICH LATER BECOMES THE INTERNET.

        Bill Gates sees the UNIVAC computer at the Seattle World's Fair.

1963   THE REVEREND MARTIN LUTHER KING, JR., GIVES HIS "I HAVE A DREAM" SPEECH IN WASHINGTON, D.C.

        U.S. PRESIDENT JOHN F. KENNEDY IS ASSASSINATED IN DALLAS, TEXAS.

1964   Melinda French is born on August 15.

1967   ISRAELI AND ARAB ARMIES ENGAGE IN THE SIX-DAY WAR.

        SOUTH AFRICAN SURGEON CHRISTIAAN BARNARD PERFORMS THE FIRST HUMAN-TO-HUMAN HEART TRANSPLANT SURGERY.

        Bill Gates starts attending Lakeside School when he is in seventh grade.

1969   U.S. ASTRONAUTS NEIL ARMSTRONG AND BUZZ ALDRIN BECOME THE FIRST TWO HUMANS TO SET FOOT ON THE MOON.

        SESAME STREET DEBUTS ON U.S. TELEVISION.

1970   THE BEATLES BREAK UP.

1971   COMPUTER ENGINEER RAY TOMLINSON SENDS THE FIRST E-MAIL.

1973   THE VIETNAM WAR COMES TO AN END.

        ISRAELI AND ARAB FORCES FIGHT AGAIN, LEADING TO AN OIL SHORTAGE IN THE UNITED STATES.

        Bill Gates works for a company called TRW in Vancouver, Washington, during his senior year of high school.

        Bill Gates starts college at Harvard University.

1975	THE FIRST VCR IS INTRODUCED BY THE SONY CORPORATION.

1975   THE FIRST VCR IS INTRODUCED BY THE SONY CORPORATION.

Bill Gates and Paul Allen sell software systems for the Altair computer to a company called MITS.

Bill Gates and Paul Allen start what will become Microsoft in Albuquerque, New Mexico.

Bill Gates leaves Harvard in his junior year.

1977   THE MOVIE *STAR WARS* IS RELEASED.

THE APPLE II COMPUTER IS INTRODUCED.

1979   A NUCLEAR POWER PLANT AT THREE MILE ISLAND, NEAR MIDDLETOWN, PENNSYLVANIA, EXPERIENCES A PARTIAL MELTDOWN.

THE WALKMAN IS INTRODUCED.

Microsoft moves to Bellevue, Washington.

1980   THE UNITED STATES AND 40 OTHER COUNTRIES BOYCOTT THE SUMMER OLYMPIC GAMES IN MOSCOW.

FORMER BEATLE JOHN LENNON IS ASSASSINATED IN NEW YORK CITY.

Microsoft signs a contract with IBM.

1981   The IBM PC is introduced.

1982   THE WORLD'S FIRST COMPACT DISC IS CREATED IN GERMANY.

Melinda French graduates from Ursuline Academy (high school).

Microsoft introduces Multiplan spreadsheet software.

1983   SALLY RIDE BECOMES THE FIRST U.S. WOMAN IN SPACE.

Microsoft introduces a word-processing program, called Word.

1985   THE NINTENDO CORPORATION INTRODUCES ITS NINTENDO ENTERTAINMENT SYSTEM.

Microsoft introduces the first Windows operating system.

1986   AN EXPLOSION ROCKS THE CHERNOBYL NUCLEAR POWER PLANT IN THE SOVIET UNION.

Microsoft stock is sold to the public.

Microsoft moves to a new corporate campus in Redmond, Washington.

1987   Melinda French graduates from Duke University and starts working at Microsoft, where she meets Bill Gates.

1989   THE BERLIN WALL FALLS IN GERMANY.

Microsoft starts the Corbis Corporation, which grows into a collection of millions of photographs and art images.

1990   Microsoft releases the electronic encyclopedia, *Encarta*.

1991   U.S. PRESIDENT GEORGE H. W. BUSH ORDERS AIR ATTACKS ON IRAQ, IN RESPONSE TO IRAQ'S PRESIDENT, SADDAM HUSSEIN, INVADING NEIGHBORING KUWAIT.

THE SOVIET UNION BREAKS UP.

1994   Bill Gates and Melinda French marry on January 1 in Hawaii.

The William H. Gates Foundation is started.

1995   *Forbes* magazine names Bill Gates "The Richest Man in the World."

Microsoft introduces its Internet browser, Explorer.

Bill Gates's book *The Road Ahead* is first published.

1996   Microsoft enters the cable news system with the MSNBC network.

Jennifer Gates is born. Melinda Gates leaves Microsoft.

1997   U.S. GOLFER TIGER WOODS BECAME THE YOUNGEST PERSON TO WIN THE FAMOUS MASTERS GOLF TOURNAMENT.

BRITISH AUTHOR J. K. ROWLING PUBLISHES THE FIRST OF HER HARRY POTTER BOOKS.

Bill, Melinda, and Jennifer Gates move into their unfinished mansion in Medina, Washington.

The Gates Library Foundation is started. Its name is changed to the Gates Learning Foundation in 1999.

1998   The U.S. government and 20 states file a lawsuit against Microsoft for unfair business practices.

1999   AFTER FEARS OF A MASS COMPUTER CRISIS, THE CHANGEOVER TO THE YEAR 2000 (OR Y2K) DOES NOT CAUSE MAJOR PROBLEMS.

Rory Gates is born.

Bill Gates's second book, *Business @ the Speed of Thought*, is published.

2000   AN E-MAIL MESSAGE WITH THE SUBJECT LINE "ILOVEYOU" RELEASES A COMPUTER VIRUS THAT DESTROYS FILES, ACCESSES LOGIN NAMES AND PASSWORDS, AND SENDS THE INFORMATION BACK TO THE CREATOR OF THE VIRUS, AFFECTING MILLIONS OF PEOPLE.

          The different Gates foundations are merged into the Bill and Melinda Gates Foundation.

          Microsoft is ordered by a U.S. judge to split into two companies. Microsoft appeals the decision.

2001   TERRORISTS ATTACK THE UNITED STATES BY HIJACKING AND CRASHING AIRPLANES INTO THE WORLD TRADE CENTER AND THE PENTAGON. OVER 3,000 PEOPLE ARE KILLED.

          After an appeal, Microsoft reaches a settlement in its unfair practices case.

2002   Microsoft releases the Xbox games system.

          Phoebe Gates is born.

2003   THE UNITED STATES DECLARES WAR ON IRAQ, CLAIMING THAT IRAQI PRESIDENT SADDAM HUSSEIN IS ON THE PATH TO USING WEAPONS OF MASS DESTRUCTION.

2004   A MASSIVE EARTHQUAKE IN THE INDIAN OCEAN CAUSES THE WORST TSUNAMI DISASTER IN HISTORY.

2005   HURRICANE KATRINA RIPS THROUGH THE U.S. GULF COAST, DESTROYING TOWNS IN ALABAMA, MISSISSIPPI, AND LOUISIANA.

          Bill and Melinda Gates are chosen by *Time* magazine as "Persons of the Year" (with Bono).

2006   Bill Gates receives the James C. Morgan Global Humanitarian Award.

2007   Melinda Gates, along with former U.S. Presidents George H. W. Bush and Bill Clinton, is honored by the Save the Children organization.

          Bill Gates receives an honorary degree from Harvard University.

2008   Bill Gates steps down as Microsoft's chief software architect to work full time at the Bill and Melinda Gates Foundation.

2009   BARACK OBAMA BECOMES PRESIDENT OF THE UNITED STATES.

Glossary

appeals court court that reviews the decision of another court and can change the first decision

BASIC short for "Beginner's All-Purpose Symbolic Instruction Code," it is a computer programming language, or code

browser program people use to find information on the Internet

capitalism economic system in which private individuals or groups own land, factories, and other businesses

charitable giving help or money to needy people

chief executive officer (CEO) high-ranking member of a company who makes major decisions for the company

Cold War mostly nonviolent—or "cold"—war between the United States and its allies and the Soviet Union and its allies. The United States believed in capitalism, while the Soviet Union believed in communism. The "war" lasted from the mid-1940s to the early 1990s.

communism economic and social system in which most of the land and businesses are owned by the state or community and shared by all

developed country country that has developed a higher level of modern technology, health care, and comforts for its citizens

developing country country that does not have modern technology, health care, and comforts for its citizens

dictatorship country run by a dictator, a ruler with absolute power

engineer person who designs and makes complex products. Some engineers design computers, while others design electronic equipment.

foundation organization that gives money to causes that will help people

graphic user interface way for a computer user to make a computer perform tasks by clicking on or moving small pictures on a screen

hardware physical parts of a computer

mainframe very large, powerful computer that is often shared by many users through separate terminals

malaria disease in the blood that causes fever, chills, and sweating. It is carried and given to people by certain kinds of mosquitoes.

microcomputer small computer that uses a single microprocessor chip. Microcomputers are also called personal computers, or PCs.

microprocessor small chip that holds the "brains" of a computer

monopoly business that has complete control over a product or service

MS-DOS short for "Microsoft Disk Operating System," it is the operating system that helped Microsoft dominate the computer industry

obsessive thinking about something all the time

operating system software that controls how a computer works. The operating system lets a person tell a computer what to do.

PDP-10 short for "Programmed Data Processor," it was a kind of early minicomputer made by a company called Digital Equipment Corporation

personal computer (PC) small desktop or laptop computer that one person can use. Personal computers are also called microcomputers.

procrastinator person who puts off doing something that should be done right away

rotavirus virus that causes severe diarrhea and fever. Without proper health care, it can cause death.

royalty share of the profits paid to the owner or creator of a product

scholarship money or other aid that helps a student get an education

shareholder someone who owns shares of stock in a business

software program that tells a computer what to do

Soviet Union union of states and republics stretching through eastern Europe and Asia, with Russia as a major member. It was formed in 1922 under communist rule. By the end of 1991, all the states and republics had declared independence, and the Soviet Union ceased to exist.

stock portion of a company that a person can buy

terminal something that allows a person to interact or communicate with a computer. A terminal usually has a keyboard and screen.

time sharing agreement to share something large and expensive, such as an early generation computer. Each user pays for the hours or days of use.

vaccine drug that keeps the body from getting a disease

virus destructive computer program that is usually hidden within a "safe" program. A virus can make copies of itself, spread through many programs, and perform harmful tasks such as destroying data.

word processing way to use a computer to create documents, such as letters, reports, and books. Word-processing software allows the user to easily type and edit.

Notes on Sources

GREAT WEALTH AND GREAT RESPONSIBILITY (PAGES 6–7)

1. Patricia Sellers, "Melinda Gates Goes Public," *Fortune*, January 7, 2008, 1.

2. Melinda French Gates (speech, SBRI Passport to Global Health Celebration, April 30, 2008),
http://www.gatesfoundation.org/speeches-commentary/Pages/melinda-french-gates-2008-sbri.aspx.

3. Bill and Melinda Gates Foundation, "Foundation Fact Sheet," http://www.gatesfoundation.org/about/Pages/foundation-fact-sheet.aspx.

4. Sellers, "Melinda Gates Goes Public," 1.

5. Bill Gates, "A New Era of Technical Leadership at Microsoft" (speech, Redmond, WA, June 15, 2006),
http://www.microsoft.com/presspass/exec/billg/speeches/2006/06-15transition.mspx.

GETTING STARTED (PAGES 10–17)

1. Janet Lowe, *Bill Gates Speaks* (New York: John Wiley & Sons, 1998), 2.

2. Stephen Manes and Paul Andrews, *Gates: How Microsoft's Mogul Reinvented an Industry—and Made Himself the Richest Man in America* (New York: Doubleday, 1993), 11–13.

3. Microsoft, "Bill Gates: Chairman," http://www.microsoft.com/presspass/exec/billg/bio.mspx?pf=true.

4. Manes and Andrews, *Gates*, 15–19; Lowe, *Bill Gates Speaks*, 2.

5. *World Book*, 1996 ed., s.v. "Computers"; *Encarta*, s.v. "UNIVAC," http://encarta.msn.com/encyclopedia_761587962/UNIVAC.html.

6. *Official Guide Book*, Seattle World's Fair, quoted in Manes and Andrews, *Gates*, 15; "50th Anniversary of UNIVAC I," *CNN.com*, June 14, 2001,
http://archives.cnn.com/2001/TECH/industry/06/14/computing.anniversary/;
University of Washington Libraries Digital Collections,
"Univac Computer, American Library Association Exhibit, Century 21 Exhibition, 1962," http://content.lib.washington.edu/cdm4/item_viewer.php?CISOROOT=/seattle&CISOPTR=2390; University of South Carolina School of Library and Information Science, "History of Information Science: 1960," http://www.libsci.sc.edu/BOB/istchron/ISCNET/ISC1960.HTM.

7. Winda Benedetti, "The Future Isn't What They Thought It Would Be Back in 1962," *Seattle Post-Intelligencer*, April 18, 2002, http://seattlepi.nwsource.com/lifestyle/66879_fairfuture.shtml.

8. Sellers, "Melinda Gates Goes Public," 1; NationMaster.com, "Melinda Gates," http://www.nationmaster.com/encyclopedia/Melinda-Gates.

9. James Wallace and Jim Erickson, *Hard Drive: Bill Gates and the Making of the Microsoft Empire* (New York: John Wiley & Sons, 1992), 12.

10. Manes and Andrews, Gates, 20–22; Michael A. Schuman, *Bill Gates: Computer Mogul and Philanthropist* (Berkeley Heights, NJ: Enslow, 2008), 83.

11. Manes and Andrews, *Gates*, 20–22; Schuman, *Computer Mogul*, 83.

12. Bill Gates, remarks at the presentation of the James C. Morgan Global Humanitarian Award (speech, San Jose, CA, November 15, 2006),
http://www.microsoft.com/presspass/exec/billg/speeches/2006/11-15TechMuseum.mspx.

13. O. Casey Corr, "Melinda French Gates: A Microsoft Mystery—She Married High-Profile Bill Gates, But Wants Her Life Kept Private," *Seattle Times*, June 4, 1995,
http://community.seattletimes.nwsource.com/archive/?date=19950604&slug=2124492.

SCHOOL DAYS (PAGES 20–27)

1. Manes and Andrews, *Gates*, 23–24; Robert Sullivan, "The Rich and How Their Kids Are Just Like Them," *New York Times*, November 19, 1995,
http://query.nytimes.com/gst/fullpage.html?res=9E06E6D91239F93AA25752C1A963958260&sec=&spon=&pagewanted=all; Wallace and Erickson, *Hard Drive*, 36–37.

2. Wallace and Erickson, *Hard Drive*, 20–22.

3. Manes and Andrews, *Gates*, 24–27.

4. Bill Gates, *The Road Ahead, Completely Revised and Up-to-Date* (New York: Penguin, 1996), 1–2.

5. Gates, *The Road Ahead*, 11; Wallace and Erickson, *Hard Drive*, 21.

6. Manes and Andrews, *Gates*, 29–32.

7. Manes and Andrews, *Gates*, 29–32.

8. Wallace and Erickson, *Hard Drive*, 35.

9. Wallace and Erickson, *Hard Drive*, 35.

10. Schuman, *Computer Mogul*, 26–32; Aaron Boyd, *Smart Money: The Story of Bill Gates* (Greensboro, NC: Morgan Reynolds, 1995), 26–27; Manes and Andrews, *Gates*, 40.

11. *World Book*, 1996 ed., s.v. "Computers."

12. Manes and Andrews, *Gates*, 51; Gates, *The Road Ahead*, 13.

13. Gates, *The Road Ahead*, 12–14.

14. Gates, *The Road Ahead*, 12–14.

15. *Seattle Times*, May 30, 1972, quoted in Manes and Andrews, *Gates*, 45–46.

HEADING TO HARVARD (PAGES 30–41)

1. Wallace and Erickson, *Hard Drive*, 36–40.

2. Wallace and Erickson, *Hard Drive*, 48–51; Manes and Andrews, *Gates*, 53.

3. Boyd, *Smart Money*, 37; Manes and Andrews, *Gates*, 53–54.

4. Manes and Andrews, *Gates*, 53–54 (from Bill Gates, interview, July 23, 1991).

5. Manes and Andrews, *Gates*, 55.

6. Manes and Andrews, *Gates*, 51.

7. Manes and Andrews, *Gates*, 54 (from Paul Allen, interview, October 31, 1991).

8. Manes and Andrews, *Gates*, 58 (from Doug Gordon, interview, September 16, 1991).

9. Gates, *The Road Ahead*, 43–44.

10. Schuman, *Computer Mogul*, 38; Manes and Andrews, *Gates*, 58–59.

11. Wallace and Erickson, *Hard Drive*, 57.

12. Corr, "Melinda French Gates."

13. Gates, *The Road Ahead*, 12–15.

14. Gates, *The Road Ahead*, 16–17.

15. Gates, *The Road Ahead*, 16–17.

16. Gates, *The Road Ahead*, 43–44; Manes and Andrews, *Gates*, 102; Wallace and Erickson, *Hard Drive*, 54.

17. Gates, *The Road Ahead*, 16–17.

18. Ed Roberts, "Electronic Desk Calculator You Can Build," *Popular Electronics*, November 1971, 27–32; Manes and Andrews, *Gates*, 67–68.

19. PC History.org, "MITS Altair 8800," http://www.pc-history.org/altair.htm.

20. Wallace and Erickson, *Hard Drive*, 73–76.

21. Gates, *The Road Ahead*, 18.

22. Bill Gates, interview by David Allison, 1993, http://americanhistory.si.edu/collections/comphist/gates.htm#tc1; Wallace and Erickson, *Hard Drive*, 79–80; Manes and Andrews, *Gates*, 70–76.

23. Gates, *The Road Ahead*, 18.

24. Craig Peters, *Bill Gates: Software Genius of Microsoft* (Berkeley Heights, NJ: Enslow, 2003), 18; Wallace and Erickson, *Hard Drive*, 83–85; and Schuman, *Computer Mogul*, 50.

25. Bill Gates, column, *New York Times Syndicate*, May 8, 1996, quoted in Lowe, *Bill Gates Speaks*, 20.

26 Wallace and Erickson, *Hard Drive*, 91; Schuman, *Computer Mogul*, 54; Gates, *The Road Ahead*, 45; Bill Gates, interview by David Allison.

PROMISES FOR THE PC (PAGES 44–55)

1. Sellers, "Melinda Gates Goes Public," 2.

2. Bill Gates, interview by David Allison; Wallace and Erickson, *Hard Drive*, 107; Manes and Andrews, *Gates*, 144.

3. Manes and Andrews, *Gates*, 129.

4. Manes and Andrews, *Gates*, 143; Microsoft PressPass, "Steve Ballmer," http://www.microsoft.com/presspass/exec/steve/?tab=biography.

5. *Encarta*, s.v. "International Business Machines Corporation," http://encarta.msn.com/encyclopedia_761587962/UNIVAC.html.

6. Gates, *The Road Ahead*, 48.

7. Gates, *The Road Ahead*, 4.

8. Manes and Andrews, *Gates*, 149; Bill Gates, interview by David Allison.

9. Schuman, *Computer Mogul*, 62–67.

10. Manes and Andrews, *Gates*, 160.

11. Schuman, *Computer Mogul*, 62–67.

12. Joan D. Dickinson, *Bill Gates: Billionaire Computer Genius* (Springfield, NJ: Enslow, 1997), 41.

13. Schuman, *Computer Mogul*, 62–67.

14. Manes and Andrews, *Gates*, 172.

15. IBM, "Personal Computer Announced by IBM," August 12, 1981, http://www-03.ibm.com/ibm/history/exhibits/pc25/pc25_press.html.

16. Computermuseum.li, "IBM Personal Computer (1981)," http://www.computermuseum.li/Testpage/IBMPC-1982.htm; IBM, "Product Fact Sheet," August 12, 1981, http://www-03.ibm.com/ibm/history/exhibits/pc25/pc25_fact.html; Dan Gookin, PCs for Dummies, 9th ed. (Indianapolis: Wiley, 2003), 151–63.

17. Peters, *Software Genius*, 20–21.

18. Gates, *The Road Ahead*, 39.

19. Cover, *Time*, January 3, 1983, http://www.time.com/time/covers/0,16641,19830103,00.html.

20. Wallace and Erickson, *Hard Drive*, 272–74.

21. Timothy Egan, "The 6.5 Billion Dollar Man," *New York Times*, October 29, 1995, http://query.nytimes.com/gst/fullpage.html?res=990CE2DA1638F93AA15753C1A9639 58260&scp=1&sq=Allen&st=nyt; Biography.com, "Paul Allen," www.biography.com/search/article.do?id=9542239&page=print.

22. Chuck Davis, "Tod Leiweke: Paul Allen's Minority Ownership Representative for the Seattle Sounders FC," *Soccer Seattle Style*, October 6, 2008, http://soccerseattlestyle.com/wp/?p=710; Wallace and Erickson, *Hard Drive*, 46.

23. Sellers, "Melinda Gates Goes Public," 2.

24. Corr, "Melinda French Gates."

25. Wallace and Erickson, *Hard Drive*, 337–38; Walter Isaacson, "In Search of the Real Bill Gates," *Time*, October 20, 2005, 11–12, http://www.time.com/time/magazine/article/0,9171,1120657,00.html.

FRIENDLIER COMPUTERS (PAGES 58–65)

1. Kevin Maney, "Apple's 1984 Super Bowl Commercial Still Stands as Watershed Event," *USA Today*, January 28, 2004, http://www.usatoday.com/tech/columnist/kevinmaney/2004-01-28-maney_x.htm.

2. Dickinson, *Billionaire Computer Genius*, 48.

3. "Microsoft Corporation," *New York Times.com*, business section company profiles, http://topics.nytimes.com/top/news/business/companies/microsoft_corporation/index.htm.

4. Gates, *The Road Ahead*, 58–59; Wallace and Erickson, Hard Drive, 252–63, 267–70; Dana Meachen Rau, *Bill and Melinda Gates* (Ann Arbor, MI: Cherry Lake, 2008), 20.

5. Wallace and Erickson, *Hard Drive*, 271.

6. Cover and Michael Moritz, Alexander L. Taylor III, and Peter Stoler, "The Wizard Inside the Machine," *Time*, April 16, 1984, http://www.time.com/time/magazine/article/0,9171,954266,00.html.

7. Isaccson, "In Search of, " 6.

8. Bill Gates, interview by David Allison; Manes and Andrews, *Gates*, 308–9.

9. Issacson, "In Search of," 9.

10. Schuman, *Computer Mogul*, 82.

11. Dickinson, *Billionaire Computer Genius*, 54–56.

12. Schuman, *Computer Mogul*, 114–15.

13. Bill and Melinda Gates Foundation, "Melinda French Gates," http://www.gatesfoundation.org/leadership/Pages/melinda-gates.aspx.

14. Sellers, "Melinda Gates Goes Public," 2.

15. Sellers, "Melinda Gates Goes Public," 2.

16. Corr, "Melinda French Gates."

17. Corr, "Melinda French Gates."

18. Kristi Heim, "Melinda Gates Urges Girls to Find Ways to Save the World," *Seattle Times,* May 24, 2008,
http://seattletimes.nwsource.com/cgi-bin/PrintStory.pl?document_id=2004435810&zsection; Susan Paynter, "Melinda Sees Pink over Girls and Computers," *Seattle Post-Intelligencer*, June 9, 1997,
http://seattlepi.nwsource.com/archives/1997/9706090024.asp.

19. Sellers, "Melinda Gates Goes Public," 2.

20. Corr, "Melinda French Gates."

21. Corr, "Melinda French Gates."

22. Alice Shroeder, "He's a Great Teacher and We Couldn't Stop Talking," *Financial Times.com*, September 27, 2008,
http://www.ft.com/cms/s/0/fed2ad82-8c2e-11dd-8a4c-0000779fd18c.html?nclick_check=1.

A LIFE TOGETHER (PAGES 68–79)

1. James Wallace, "Billionaire Bill Gates Marries Melinda French," *Seattle Post-Intelligencer*, January 3, 1994, http://seattlepi.nwsource.com/archives/1994/9401030044.asp; Jeryl Brunner, "Celebrity Honeymoon Escapes," USA Today, March 30, 2007,
http://www.usatoday.com/travel/destinations/2007-03-30-celebrity-honeymoons-forbes_N.htm.

2. Sellers, "Melinda Gates Goes Public," 1; Isaacson, "In Search of," 6.

3. Gates, *The Road Ahead*, 249–53; Matt Woolsey, "Homes of the Billionaires," *Forbes.com*,
http://www.forbes.com/forbeslife/2007/09/20/billionaires-homes-properties-forbeslife-richlist07-cx_mw_0920realestate_slide_2.html.

4. Woolsey, "Homes of the Billionaires"; Isaacson, "In Search of," 7.

5. Gates, *The Road Ahead*, 250–53; Cynthia Crossen, *The Rich and How They Got That Way* (New York: Crown, 2000), 234.

6. Gates, *The Road Ahead*, 258; Thane Peterson, "The Art of Being Bill Gates," Business Week, August 14, 2003; Joseph Tartakoff, "Bill Gates Discusses His Leonardo da Vinci Notebook," *Seattle Post Intelligencer*, February 12, 2007, http://blog.seattlepi.nwsource.com/microsoft/archives/111500.asp.

7. Sellers, "Melinda Gates Goes Public," 3; Isaacson, "In Search of," 12; Melinda Gates, interview by Kathi Goertzen, *KOMONews*, November 4, 2004,

http://www.komonews.com/news/archive/4137326.html.

8. "Bill Gates: My Kids Get Limited Computer Time," *Foxnews.com*, February 21, 2007,

http://www.foxnews.com/story/0,2933,253360,00.html.

9. Warren Buffet and Bill Gates, "Buffet and Gates Go Back to School," interview at the University of Nebraska School of Business Administration, September 2005.

10. Sellers, "Melinda Gates Goes Public," 2; Kalpana Jain, "Women Can Have Enormous Power: Melinda Gates," *Times of India*, January 26, 2004, http://www1.timesofindia.indiatimes.com/articleshow/445025.cms.

11. Fundinguniverse.com, "Bill and Melinda Gates," http://www.fundinguniverse.com/company-histories/Bill-amp;-Melinda-Gates-Foundation-Company-History.html; Amanda Ripley, "From Rags to Riches," *Time*, December 19, 2005,

http://www.time.com/time/magazine/article/0,9171,1142276-1,00.html.

12. Bill and Melinda Gates Foundation, "Letter from Bill and Melinda Gates," http://www.gatesfoundation.org/about/Pages/bill-melinda-gates-letter.aspx.

13. Bill Gates (speech, Public Library Association 10th National Conference, February 25, 2004),

http://www.gatesfoundation.org/speeches-commentary/Pages/bill-gates-2004-public-library-association.aspx; Fundinguniverse.com, "Bill and Melinda Gates Foundation,"

http://www.fundinguniverse.com/company-histories/Bill-amp;-Melinda-Gates-Foundation-Company-History.html.

14. Bill and Melinda Gates Foundation, "Foundation Timeline," http://www.gatesfoundation.org/about/Pages/foundation-timeline.aspx; Fundinguniverse.com, "Bill and Melinda Gates Foundation"; Bill and Melinda Gates Foundation, "Foundation Fact Sheet."

15. Gates, *The Road Ahead*, 3–5.

16. Gates, *The Road Ahead*, 111–12, x–xii; *Encarta*, s.v. "Uses of the Internet," http://encarta.msn.com/encyclopedia_761579729/Internet.html.

17. Gates, *The Road Ahead*, 111–12, xi.

18. John Heilemann, *Pride Before the Fall: The Trials of Bill Gates and the End of the Microsoft Era* (New York: HarperCollins, 2001), 16; John Borland, "Victor: Software Empire Pays High Price," *cnetnew.com*, April 15, 2003,

http://news.cnet.com/Victor-Software-empire-pays-high-price/2009-1032_3-995681.html?tag=mncol.

19. "Microsoft Corporation," *New York Times.com*.

20. "Microsoft Corporation," *New York Times.com*.

21. Joe Wilcox, "Microsoft, Feds Reach a Deal," *cnetnew.com*, November 2, 2001, http://news.cnet.com/Microsoft%2C-Feds-reach-a-deal/2100-1002_3-275317.html?tag=mncol; "Microsoft Corporation," *New York Times.com*.

A MAJOR SHIFT (PAGES 82–91)

1. Isaacson, "In Search of," 1; "Buffet and Gates Go Back to School."

2. Bill and Melinda Gates Foundation, "Guiding Principles," http://www.gatesfoundation.org/about/Pages/guiding-principles.aspx.

3. Sellers, "Melinda Gates Goes Public," 1.

4. Melinda Gates, interview by Patricia Sellers, Fortune Most Powerful Women Summit, October 3, 2008,

http://money.cnn.com/video/ft/#/video/fortune/2008/10/07/fortune.mpw.gates.schools. fortune.

5. Cecelia Goodnow, "Melinda Gates Strives for Work–Family Balance," *Seattle Post-Intelligencer*, October 18, 2003,

http://seattlepi.nwsource.com/lifestyle/144366_melinda18.htm; Patricia Sellers, "Gates, Buffett and Powerful Women," *Fortune.com*, with *CNN.com*, October 3, 2008,

http://postcards.blogs.fortune.cnn.com/2008/10/03/gates-buffett-and-powerful-women/; Sellers, "Melinda Gates Goes Public," 1.

6. Sellers, "Melinda Gates Goes Public," 3; Alexander G. Higgins, "More Togetherness Now for Bill and Melinda Gates," *Kansas City Star*, February 1, 2009,

http://www.kansascity.com/440/story/1011991.html.

7. Melinda French Gates (speech, SBRI Passport to Global Health Celebration, April 30, 2008).

8. Ripley, "From Riches to Rags"; Fundinguniverse.com, "Bill and Melinda Gates Foundation."

9. Donna Gordon Blankinship, "Melinda Gates Shares the Lessons She's Learned in 10 Years of Philanthropy," *Seattle Times*, May 1, 2007,

http://seattletimes.nwsource.com/cgi-bin/PrintStory.pl?document_id=2003687791.

10. Microsoft, "Facts about Microsoft: Subsidiaries," http://www.microsoft.com/presspass/ insidefacts_ms.mspx#EPEAC.

11. Bill and Melinda Gates Foundation, "Grand Challenges in Global Health," October 22, 2008,

http://www.grandchallenges.org/about/Newsroom/Pages/GCERound1Grants.aspx.

12. Bill and Melinda Gates Foundation, "Foundation Fact Sheet."

13. "Buffet and Gates Go Back to School"; Carol J. Loomis, "Warren Buffett Gives Away His Fortune," *Fortune*, with *CNNMoney.com*, June 25, 2006,

http://money.cnn.com/2006/06/25/magazines/fortune/charity1.fortune/index.htm.

14. Matthew Miller, "Gates No Longer World's Richest Man," *Forbes.com*, March 5, 2008,

http://www.forbes.com/billionaires/2008/03/05/buffett-worlds-richest-cx_mm_ 0229buffetrichest.html; "The Vanity Fair 100," *Vanity Fair*, October 2008, 269.

15. Bill Gates, "A New Era of Technical Leadership at Microsoft."

16. Bill Gates, "A New Era of Technical Leadership at Microsoft."

17. Bill Gates, "A New Era of Technical Leadership at Microsoft."

18. Todd Bishop, "Amid Cheers and Tears, Gates Says Goodbye," *Seattle Post Intelligence*, June 28, 2008, http://seattlepi.nwsource.com/business/368824_gatesfinal28.html.

19. Bishop, "Amid Tears."

20. Warren Buffett, interview by Carol J. Loomis, *Fortune.com*, with *CNNMoney.com*, June 25, 2006,

http://money.cnn.com/2006/06/25/magazines/fortune/charity2.fortune/index.htm; Carol. J.

Loomis, "How Buffett's Giveaway Will Work," *Fortune.com*, with *CNNMoney.com*, June 25, 2006,

   http://money.cnn.com/2006/06/25/magazines/fortune/charity3.fortune/index.htm; Ripley, "From Rags to Riches."

   21. Byron Acohido, "Bill Gates Gets Honorary Knighthood." *USA Today*, March 1, 2005,

   http://www.usatoday.com/money/industries/technology/2005-03-01-sir-bill-usat_x.htm; Savethechildren.org, "Save the Children's 75th Anniversary Benefit,"

   http://www.savethechildren.org/newsroom/2007/75th-anniversary-benefit.html;

   "The 100 Most Powerful Women," *Forbes.com*, August 31, 2006, and August 27, 2008,

   http://www.forbes.com/lists/2006/11/06women_Melinda-Gates_7UR5.html and

   http://www.forbes.com/business/lists/2008/11/biz_powerwomen08_Melinda-Gates_7UR5.html; Melinda French Gates (speech, SBRI Passport to Global Health Celebration, April 30, 2008).

   22. Bill Gates (Harvard commencement speech, June 7, 2007), http://www.news.harvard.edu/gazette/2007/06.14/99-gates.html.

   23. Bill Gates (Harvard commencement speech).

Further Reading

Aronson, Marc. *Up Close: Bill Gates*. New York: Penguin, 2008.

Boyd, Aaron. *Smart Money: The Story of Bill Gates*. Greensboro, NC: Morgan Reynolds, 2004.

Endlich, Lisa. *Be the Change*. New York: Collins Business, 2008 *(Introduction by Bill and Melinda Gates about philanthropy.)*

Ferguson's Careers in Focus. *Computers*. New York: Infobase Publishing, 2008.

Gillam, Scott. *Steve Jobs*. Edina, MN: ABDO Publishing Co., 2008.

Imbimbo, Anthony. *Steve Jobs: The Brilliant Mind Behind Apple*. Pleasantville, NY: Gareth Stevens Publishing, 2009.

Karnes, Frances, and Kristen R. Stephens. *Empowered Girls: A Girl's Guide to Positive Activism, Volunteering, and Philanthropy*. Waco, TX: Prufrock, 2005.

McLeese, Don. *The Internet and E-mail*. Vero Beach, FL: Rourke, 2009

Musolf, Nell. *The Story of Microsoft*. Mankato, MN: Creative Education, 2009.

Offinoski, Steven. *Computers*. New York: Marshall Cavendish Benchmark, 2007.

Rau, Dana Meachen. *Life Skills Biographies: Bill and Melinda Gates*. Ann Arbor, MI: Cherry Lake, 2008.

Reeves, Diane Lindsey, with Lindsey Clasen. *Career Ideas for Kids Who Like Computers*. New York: Ferguson, 2007.

Schuman, Michael A. *Bill Gates: Computer Mogul and Philanthropist*. Berkeley Heights, NJ: Enslow, 2008.

Slater, Robert. *Microsoft Rebooted: How Bill Gates and Steve Ballmer Reinvented Their Company*. New York: Portfolio, 2004.

Takahashi, Dean. *Opening the Xbox: Inside Microsoft's Plan to Unleash an Entertainment Revolution*. Roseville, CA: Prima, 2002.

Weber, Sandra. *The Personal Computer*. Philadelphia: Chelsea House Publishers, 2004.

Woodford, Chris. Communications and Computers. New York: Facts on File, Inc., 2004.

Find Out More

The Bill and Melinda Gates Foundation
www.gatesfoundation.org
> *Find out about all of the causes that Bill and Melinda Gates are supporting and bringing attention to.*

Computer History Museum
www.computerhistory.org
> *Find out about this fascinating museum dedicated to computer history. Even if you can't visit Mountain View, CA, you can still take a video tour of the museum!*

Kids Caring 4 Kids
www.kidscaring4kids.org
> *Check out this philanthropy website for students. Get involved!*

PC History website
www.pc-history.org
> *Find out about the early days of the PC, starting with the Altair 8800!*

SPEECHES
Bill and Melinda Gates give a lot of speeches. Listen to them for youself!

Bill Gates Gives Keynote Address at Lakeside School, September 23, 2005.
www.lakesideschool.org/give/campaign/BGatesKeynoteAddress.pdf

Remarks by Bill Gates at a news conference about stepping down from Microsoft, June 15, 2006.
www.microsoft.com/presspass/exec/billg/speeches/2006/06-15transition.mspx?pf=true

Remarks by Bill Gates at the Presentation of James C. Morgan Global Humanitarian Award. Tech Museum of Innovation, San Jose, California. November 15, 2006.
www.microsoft.com/presspass/exec/billg/speeches/2006/11-15TechMuseum.mspx

Remarks of Bill Gates at Harvard Commencement (in the *Harvard University Gazette* Online), June 7, 2007.
www.news.harvard.edu/gazette/2007/06.14/99-gates.html

Bill and Melinda Gates at the World Economic Forum, January 30, 2009
www.gatesfoundation.org/speeches-commentary/Pages/bill-melinda-gates-2009-world-economic-forum-speech-davos.aspx

Remarks by Melinda French Gates to SBRI Passport to Global Health Celebration. April 30, 2008.
www.gatesfoundation.org/speeches-commentary/Pages/melinda-french-gates-2008-sbri.aspx.

OTHER ARTICLES AND STORIES FOUND ONLINE:

Letter from Bill and Melinda Gates at the Gates Foundation website:
www.gatesfoundation.org/about/Pages/bill-melinda-gates-letter.aspx

Historical Press Releases and Interviews with Industry Leaders, Smithsonian National Museum of American History, Computer History Collection
www.americanhistory.si.edu/collections/comphist/

Announcement of IBM Personal Computer, August 12, 1981:
www-03.ibm.com/ibm/history/exhibits/pc25/pc25_press.html

Forbes List of the World's Billionaires:
www.forbes.com/2009/03/11/worlds-richest-people-billionaires-2009-billionaires_land.html

Index